Pensions at a Glance

PUBLIC ~~P~~ ~~C~~UNTRIES

OECD

ORGANISATION FOR ECONOMIC CO-OPERATION AND DEVELOPMENT

ORGANISATION FOR ECONOMIC CO-OPERATION AND DEVELOPMENT

The OECD is a unique forum where the governments of 30 democracies work together to address the economic, social and environmental challenges of globalisation. The OECD is also at the forefront of efforts to understand and to help governments respond to new developments and concerns, such as corporate governance, the information economy and the challenges of an ageing population. The Organisation provides a setting where governments can compare policy experiences, seek answers to common problems, identify good practice and work to co-ordinate domestic and international policies.

The OECD member countries are: Australia, Austria, Belgium, Canada, the Czech Republic, Denmark, Finland, France, Germany, Greece, Hungary, Iceland, Ireland, Italy, Japan, Korea, Luxembourg, Mexico, the Netherlands, New Zealand, Norway, Poland, Portugal, the Slovak Republic, Spain, Sweden, Switzerland, Turkey, the United Kingdom and the United States. The Commission of the European Communities takes part in the work of the OECD.

OECD Publishing disseminates widely the results of the Organisation's statistics gathering and research on economic, social and environmental issues, as well as the conventions, guidelines and standards agreed by its members.

> *This work is published on the responsibility of the Secretary-General of the OECD. The opinions expressed and arguments employed herein do not necessarily reflect the official views of the Organisation or of the governments of its member countries.*

Also available in French under the title:
Les pensions dans les pays de l'OCDE
PANORAMA DES POLITIQUES PUBLIQUES

Foreword

This report provides indicators for comparing pension policies across OECD countries. It looks at the main features of pension systems, such as contribution rates to defined-contribution schemes, accrual rates in earnings-related schemes, ceilings to pensionable earnings and indexation of pensions in payment.

Based on the parameters and rules of 2002 (but including legislated changes that are phased in over time), future pension entitlements are calculated for workers starting their careers today.

Pension entitlements are shown on both a gross and a net basis taking into account taxes and social security contributions paid by workers and pensioners. The results cover all mandatory parts of the retirement-income system, including resource-tested benefits, basic pensions, as well as public and compulsory private pension schemes.

Comprehensive policy indicators are also developed of the cost of countries' pension promises, the potential resource transfer to pensioners and the structure of the pension package.

Country Studies (Part II) provide a summary of each country's pension system and include detailed country-specific results.

This report was prepared by Monika Queisser of the Social Policy Division of the Directorate for Employment, Labour and Social Affairs, and Edward Whitehouse, a consultant to the OECD and director of Axia Economics, London. Gordon Keenay assisted with the analysis of the tax position of pensioners. David Stanton provided guidance in the early stages of the project. National officials provided invaluable active assistance in collecting information on their countries' pension and tax systems.

Delegates to the OECD Working Party on Social Policy advised on modelling procedures and development of indicators for cross-country comparison of pension systems. They also gave constructive comments on earlier drafts of the report.

The OECD pension models build on those originally developed by Axia Economics with the help of funding from the Directorate of Employment, Labour and Social Affairs, the Directorate of Financial and Enterprise Affairs and the Economics Department of the OECD. Further development of this modelling approach was supported by other organisations, including the World Bank, and the International Association of Pension Fund Managers (FIAP).

Table of Contents

Part II
Country Studies

PENSIONS AT A GLANCE – ISBN 92-64-01871-9 – © OECD 2005

List of Box

List of Tables

List of Figures

Preface: Why Pensions at a Glance?

Reforming pensions is one of the biggest challenges of the century. All OECD countries have to adjust to the ageing of their populations and re-balance retirement income provision to keep it *adequate* and ensure that the retirement income system is financially *sustainable*. Demographers have been warning us for some time that ageing is looming and that when it strikes populations and workforces will rapidly age. But many governments preferred to ignore the call for reform and cling to the hope of postponing solutions beyond the next election or claiming that rather painless remedies could be found. Immigration of younger workers, more women in work and higher productivity were put forward in the hope that more painful solutions could be avoided. All of these factors can certainly help to cope with ageing and especially with the financing of pensions but the increases necessary to compensate for ageing are so large that one cannot rely on them alone.

Most OECD countries have realised this and have undertaken numerous reforms during past years. But pension reform is a difficult task. It involves long-term policy decisions under uncertain conditions and often the likely impact of these decisions on the well-being of pensioners is not spelt out clearly. More than most other areas, pension reform is a highly sensitive topic. Not only does it lead to heated ideological debates, but it makes people protest in the streets, and even forces governments to retreat from needed reforms.

As people working on pension reforms around the world, we at the OECD Secretariat are asked time and again for the "right" solution to the problem. Which country does it the best way, which country is doing the worst job, which systems are the most generous, will it be possible to reform without increasing pensioner poverty, and will countries be able to pay for the promises they are making?

There are no simple answers to these questions. National retirement-income systems are complex and pension benefits depend on a wide range of factors. Differences in retirement ages, benefit calculation methods and adjustment of paid-out pensions make it very difficult to compare pension policies across countries. Another problem is that life expectancies at retirement differ from one country to another, which means that some countries will have to pay pensions for a much longer period of retirement than others. As a result national debates are often full of misleading claims regarding the generosity and affordability of other countries' pension arrangements.

International comparisons to date have focussed mostly on the fiscal aspects of the ageing problem. The OECD has also published projections of age-related expenditures including public pensions (see the June 2001 issue of the *Economic Outlook* for details). But much less attention has been paid to the social sustainability of pension systems and the impact of reforms on the adequacy and distribution of pensioner incomes. But these aspects are also crucial if countries want to attain the dual objective of promising affordable pensions and preventing a resurgence of pensioner poverty.

This report presents the first direct comparison of pension promises across OECD countries. It provides a novel framework to assess the future impact of today's pension policies, including their economic and social objectives. It takes account of the detailed rules of pension systems but summarises them in measures that are easy to compare. Pension benefits are projected for workers at different levels of earnings, covering all mandatory sources of retirement income for private-sector workers, including minimum pensions, basic and means-tested schemes, earnings-related programmes and defined contribution schemes. Another novelty is the inclusion of the large effects of the personal income tax and social security contributions on living standards in work and in retirement: all indicators are presented *gross* and *net* of taxes and contributions.

The framework can be used in different ways. As it is flexible to changing assumptions, the impact of policy reforms and economic developments on pension entitlements can be simulated. It can provide answers to questions such as what would happen if a country switched from wage to price indexation of pensions, or changed the benefit accrual rate. It can also inform on the impact of changes in economic growth, interest rates, wage growth or inflation on pensions of future retirees. The OECD will use the framework to monitor pension reforms in member countries by updating this report regularly. This report is the first in a biennial series which will be produced in co-operation with the European Commission.

Public opinion on pensions is changing. People are realising that a shrinking number of young workers will have trouble paying for more and more pensioners. Time has come to open a frank debate among all members of society and address the question of how the cost of ageing should be distributed in each society. Our publication aims to contribute to this debate by shedding more light on the social and economic implications of pension reform.

John Martin
Director of the OECD Employment,
Labour and Social Affairs Directorate

Introduction

National retirement-income systems are complex and diverse. As a result, comparing them across countries is difficult.

Cross-country analysis of pension systems has typically taken three forms:

- An *institutional* approach consisting of: descriptions of schemes' structures, rules and parameters. One example is the biennial reports, published as *Social Security Programmes throughout the World* by the United States Social Security Administration and the International Social Security Association. Another is the Mutual Information System on Social Security (Missoc) produced by the European Commission.

- An *income-distribution* analysis: using household survey data to assess the incomes of older people relative to the population as a whole. An example is the OECD's latest income-distribution analysis, published as Förster and Mira d'Ercole (2005). Disney and Whitehouse (2001, 2003) provide a survey of cross-country studies of older people's economic well being.

- A financial and *fiscal* analysis: projecting pension expenditures into the future (typically public expenditures alone). The OECD has regularly produced such projections for its member countries, the latest published as Dang *et al.* (2001).

Each of these traditional methods of cross-country analysis of pension systems has its disadvantages.

The first – institutional analysis – is an essential part of making international comparisons, but is very difficult to use as the basis for policy comparisons given the level of detail involved.

The second – income-distribution analysis – is backward-looking. The economic well-being of today's older people depends on the rules of the pension system in the past. These have been in constant flux. Monitoring and analysing pension policy needs to focus on the rules of today's systems. Their effects – on contributors and beneficiaries, and on the economy as a whole – will be felt for decades to come.

The third – financial projections – tends to focus only on *public* pension spending, ignoring the broader range of resource transfers to older people. Furthermore, such projections must implicitly be based on aggregation of individual pension entitlements, but in practice the micro-foundations are often weak. While the public-finance implications of ageing societies are undeniably important, they are not the only measure of the "problem" of ageing populations. First, low public transfers might be more sustainable than higher ones in the sense that the public finance implication are easier to manage. But, if the level of transfers is too low, the social consequences will inevitably call the underlying system into question. Second, measures of the aggregate level of transfers tell us nothing about how these transfers are distributed across beneficiaries.

This report adopts a fourth approach: microeconomic projections of pension benefits for workers at different levels of earnings. As such, its aim is to provide the means to assess the broad impact of pension policies, including both their economic and social objectives.

This approach has many advantages:*

● Like the institutional approach, it takes account of the detailed rules of pension systems but summarises them in measures that are easy to compare across countries.

● It is forward looking, assessing the future implications of today's pension policies. It does not confuse the situation of current retirees and those approaching retirement with the long-run stance of the pension system.

● It is "decomposable". Its primary aim is to assess the parameters and rules of the pension system without the "noise" of other influences. The effects of countries' demographic profile, macroeconomic aggregates, earnings distribution, etc. can be isolated both from one another and from pension policy choices.

Furthermore, this microeconomic technique, which has been applied to all 30 OECD member countries, is:

● comprehensive and adaptable, since it covers all mandatory sources of retirement income for private-sector workers, including minimum pensions, basic and means-tested schemes, earnings-related programmes and defined-contribution schemes;

● novel, since it includes new indicators of the average generosity of pension schemes, of the scale and structure of the potential resource transfer to older people and of the progressivity of pension benefit formulae;

● broad, covering the full earnings range from low- to high-income workers;

● flexible to assumptions, such as economic variables (inflation, interest rates, real earnings growth) or parameters (*e.g.*, what would happen if a country switched from wage to price indexation of pensions, or changed the accrual rate, etc.); and

● inclusive, since it also allows for the large effects of the personal income tax and social security contributions on living standards in work and in retirement (which is often ignored, especially in cross-country analyses).

The structure of this report is as follows. The first chapter gives a typology of pension systems. The intention here is not to classify countries; rather it is to give an indication of which countries have which features in their mandatory pension systems.

In Chapter 2, this framework is filled out with cross-country comparisons of the parameters and rules of all types of pension schemes. There is also information on the treatment of pensioners and pension incomes under the personal income tax and social security contributions.

The third chapter outlines the methodology and the assumptions that have to be made to generate comparative information on pension entitlements. (The sensitivity of the results to assumptions is examined in Annex I.2.)

---

* There have been a number of previous studies that share this report's aim of calculating pension entitlements for illustrative workers, such as Eurostat (1993), Aldrich (1982), and McHale (1999) and Disney and Johnson (2001). Some have ignored private pension benefits or treated them only cursorily. Some have ignored the effect of income taxes and social security contributions and looked only at gross pension entitlements.

The remaining chapters contain comparative information on pension benefits. Chapters 4 and 5 present the main results on pension entitlements across countries. Chapters 6 and 7 extend the analysis to provide more comprehensive indicators that are of most use in monitoring pension policies.

Finally, the country studies (Part II) describe national pension systems and provide further country-specific results on pension entitlements.

ISBN 92-64-01871-9
Pensions at a Glance
Public Policies across OECD Countries
© OECD 2005

Executive Summary

Recent years have seen a wave of pension reforms across OECD countries. These changes were motivated primarily by concerns about the *financial sustainability* of pension systems in the context of ageing populations. An in-depth look at pension systems reveals complex structures and rules, which make it difficult to compare retirement-income regimes. Nevertheless, sharing experience of pension reform and its impact provides valuable information for policy makers.

The report shows how large a pension people who start work now can expect to receive when they retire. This analysis answers a number of policy questions. Do retirement-income systems protect against poverty? Are they financially sustainable? How do they treat people who have low incomes or time out of employment? The report is the first in a series that will appear every two years. Future editions will also assess the impact of pension reforms.

This report shows the direction in which pension systems are heading. The cross-country comparisons reveal a diversity of pension provision in OECD countries. The analysis presented in this report covers all mandatory pension schemes – not only public pension systems, but also all compulsory private pensions. It also examines safety-nets for the elderly, and it takes account of differences in taxes, both across countries and between workers and pensioners. As such, this report provides a complete picture of the transfers across and within generations, and thus of the *social adequacy* of pension systems. Pension programmes have two main objectives. The first is redistribution of income towards low-income pensioners and prevention of destitution in old age. The second is helping workers maintain living standards during retirement by replacing income from work at an adequate level. Most countries pursue both goals in their overall pension policy, but there is large variation in the balance of emphasis between the two each objectives.

This report shows that workers on average earnings in OECD countries can expect their post-tax pension to be worth just under 70% of their earnings after tax. The countries with the lowest *net replacement rate* are Ireland and New Zealand, which have just basic pension schemes and net replacement rates of less than 40%. The United Kingdom and the United States have slightly higher net replacement rates of around 50%.

Low-income workers in OECD countries on half of average earnings will receive a net replacement rate on average of about 85%. But pensions for poor workers are very low in some countries. In Germany, Mexico, the Slovak Republic and the United States, safety-net pensions for full-career workers are worth less than a quarter of economy-wide average earnings.

Some countries have aimed to *link contributions and benefits* more closely. In Italy, Poland and Hungary, for example, the redistributive features of pension systems have been all but eliminated. If the pension system does not redistribute to poorer people, then means-tested safety-net provisions will generally play a more prominent role in retirement incomes.

All OECD countries have some form of *safety-net* for older people. Usually, these are means-tested programmes. The average minimum retirement benefit for full-career workers across OECD countries is worth a little under 29% of average earnings.

This report reveals that the personal *tax system* plays an important role in old-age support. Pensioners often do not pay social security contributions and, as personal income taxes are progressive, the average tax rate on pension income is typically less than the tax rate on earned income. In addition, most income tax systems give preferential treatment either to pension incomes or to pensioners, by giving additional allowances or credits to older people.

Net replacement rates at average earnings are 22% larger than gross replacement rates (averaging across the OECD). However, the effect of taxes and contributions on low earners is more muted than on average because the former pay less in taxes and contribution than higher-income workers. The differential between gross and net replacement rates for low earners is 17% on average.

Most countries withdraw tax concessions from richer pensioners. However, Germany and the United States are two exceptions. They provide tax concessions across the income range (although this is changing in Germany).

The adjustment of pensions in payment to reflect changes in costs or standards of living – "*indexation*" – has long been central to the debate on the financial sustainability of pension systems. Nearly all OECD countries now link pensions to consumer prices. However, some still adjust pensions in line with average earnings, which may cost more than 20% more than if pensions were indexed to prices.

A related feature is "*valorisation*": the adjustment of past earnings to account for changes in living standards between the time when pension rights are earned and when they are claimed. Until very recently, valorisation has received much less attention than indexation despite its powerful impact on pension benefits.

Most OECD countries revalue past earnings in line with economy-wide earnings growth. But there are several exceptions – Belgium, France, Korea, and Spain – where past earnings are valorised with prices. Wages usually grow faster than prices, so price valorisation leads to substantially lower replacement rates than earnings valorisation. Price valorisation for a full-career could result in a pension 40% lower than under earnings valorisation.

Pension wealth – the present value of the future stream of pension payments – is the most comprehensive indicator of pension promises. It takes into account the level at which pensions are paid, the age at which people become eligible to receive a pension, people's life expectancy and how pensions are adjusted after retirement to reflect growth in wages or prices. Luxembourg has the highest pension wealth for a worker who earned average earnings, worth 18 times average earnings for men and nearly 22 times for women (due to higher female life expectancy). This is equivalent to USD 587 000 at the time of retirement, nearly treble the average for OECD countries. The lowest pension wealth for someone who has earned average earnings when working is found in Ireland, Mexico, New Zealand, the United Kingdom and the United States, where it is less than six times average earnings.

The *pension eligibility age* in most OECD countries is 65. Iceland and Norway have and the United States will have a normal pension age of 67. Pension eligibility ages are less than 65 in the Czech Republic, France, Hungary, Korea, the Slovak Republic and Turkey. France has gross replacement rates below the OECD average at earnings between 75 and 200% of the average. Pension wealth, however, exceeds the OECD average because the pension eligibility age of 60 is relatively low and life expectancy is relatively long.

The impact of differences in *life expectancy* on pension wealth is quite large. Other things being equal, the countries with low life expectancy – Hungary, Mexico, Poland, the Slovak Republic and Turkey – could afford to pay men a pension 10% higher than a country with OECD average mortality rates (Germany, Italy and the United Kingdom, for example). In contrast, longer life expectancies increase the burden on the pension system. For men, pension wealth is nearly 8% higher in the five countries with the longest life expectancy, which are Japan, Iceland, Norway, Sweden and Switzerland.

PART I

Monitoring Pension Policies

This part contains the comparative analysis of pension entitlements. The first chapter gives a typology of pension systems that shows the main features of mandatory pension systems in the 30 OECD countries. In Chapter 2, this framework is filled out with cross-country comparisons of the parameters and rules of all types of pension schemes. There is also information on the treatment of pensioners and pension incomes under the personal income tax and social security contributions. Chapter 3 outlines the methodology and the assumptions that have to be made to generate comparative information on pension entitlements. The remaining chapters contain comparative information on pension benefits. Chapters 4 and 5 present the main results on pension entitlements across countries. Chapters 6 and 7 extend the analysis to provide more comprehensive indicators that are of most use in monitoring pension policies. Finally, the country studies (Part II) describe national pension systems and provide further country-specific results on pension entitlements.

ISBN 92-64-01871-9
Pensions at a Glance
Public Policies across OECD Countries
© OECD 2005

PART I

Chapter 1

Pension-system Typology

There have been numerous typologies of retirement-income systems. The terminology used in these categorisations has become very confusing. Perhaps the most commonly-used typology is the World Bank's "three-pillar" classification (World Bank, 1994), between "a publicly managed system with mandatory participation and the limited goal of reducing poverty among the old [first pillar]; a privately managed mandatory savings system [second pillar]; and voluntary savings [third pillar]". But this is a prescriptive rather than a descriptive typology. Subsequent analysts have allocated all public pension programmes to the first pillar. This has included earnings-related public schemes, which certainly do not meet the original definition of the first pillar. The most recent addition is the concept of a "zero pillar", comprising non-contributory schemes aimed at alleviating poverty among older people. But this is rather closer to the original description of a first pillar.

The OECD has developed a taxonomy that avoids the concept of pillars altogether. It aims, instead, for a global classification for pension plans, pension funds and pension entities that is descriptive and consistent over a range of countries with different retirement-income systems (OECD, 2004).

The approach adopted here follows this line. It is based on the role and objective of each part of the pension system. The framework has two mandatory tiers: a redistributive part and an insurance part. Redistributive components of pension systems are designed to ensure that pensioners achieve some absolute, minimum standard of living. Insurance components are designed to achieve some target standard of living in retirement compared with that when working. Voluntary provision, be it individual or employer-provided, makes up a third tier. Within these tiers, schemes are classified further by their form (public or private, defined benefit or defined contribution). This typology therefore clearly separates form from function, and description from prescription. Table 1.1 summarises the systems of the 30 OECD member countries divided into the redistributive first tier and the insurance second tier.

1. First-tier, redistributive pensions

All OECD countries have safety-nets in place that aim to prevent poverty of the elderly. These schemes, called "first-tier, redistributive schemes" here, can be of four different types: social assistance, separate targeted retirement-income programmes, basic pension schemes and minimum pensions within earnings-related plans. All of these are provided by the public sector and are mandatory.

In basic pension schemes, the benefit is either flat-rate, i.e., the same amount is paid to every retiree, or it depends only on years of work (but not on past earnings). Additional income from other sources does not change the entitlement to the basic pension. Eleven countries have a basic pension scheme.[1]

Targeted plans, in contrast, pay a higher benefit to poorer pensioners and reduced benefits to better-off retirees. The targeting takes three different forms. First, benefits can be pension-income tested (where the value depends only on the level of pension income a

Table 1.1. **Structure of pension systems in OECD countries**

Tier: function	First tier: universal coverage, redistributive				Second tier: mandatory, insurance		
Provision	Public				Public	Private	
Type	Social assistance	Targeted	Basic	Minimum	Type	DB	DC
Australia		✓					✓
Austria		✓			DB		
Belgium		✓		✓	DB		
Canada		✓	✓		DB		
Czech Republic	✓		✓	✓	DB		
Denmark		✓	✓		DB/DC		✓
Finland		✓			DB		
France		✓		✓	DB + points		
Germany	✓				Points		
Greece		✓		✓	DB		
Hungary				✓	DB		✓
Iceland		✓				✓	
Ireland		✓	✓				
Italy	✓				Notional ac		
Japan			✓		DB		
Korea		✓			DB		
Luxembourg	✓		✓	✓	DB		
Mexico		✓					✓
Netherlands	✓		✓			✓	
New Zealand			✓				
Norway		✓	✓		Points		
Poland				✓	Notional ac		✓
Portugal	✓			✓	DB		
Slovak Republic				✓	Points		
Spain				✓	DB		
Sweden		✓			Notional ac	✓	✓
Switzerland		✓		✓	DB	Defined credit	
Turkey		✓		✓	DB		
United Kingdom		✓	✓	✓	DB		
United States		✓			DB		

DB: Defined benefit.

DC: Defined contribution.

Notes on first-tier schemes: Social assistance refers to general programmes that also cover older people. Targeted covers specific schemes for older people that are resource-tested. Basic schemes are either universal, flat-rate programmes or pay a flat amount per year of coverage. Minimum pensions are redistributive parts of earnings-related schemes.

Notes on second-tier schemes: Includes quasi-mandatory schemes with broad coverage. France has two programmes: the public scheme and mandatory occupational plans. Denmark's scheme is a hybrid of DB and DC.

Source: Based on information provided by national authorities.

retiree receives), broader-income tested (reducing payments if, for example, a retiree has income from savings) or broader means-tested (reducing the pension to take account of both income and assets). There are 18 OECD countries with this type of pension programme.[2]

Minimum pensions are similar to targeted plans since they also aim to prevent pensions from falling below a certain level. But the institutional set-up and the eligibility conditions are different. Minimum pensions, as they are defined here, are part of the rules of the second-tier, earnings-related pension provision. Usually, retirees must have paid contributions for a minimum number of years in order to receive this benefit. Minimum credits in earnings-related schemes, such as those in Belgium and the United Kingdom, have a similar effect: benefits for workers with very low earnings are calculated as if the worker had earned at a higher level.

Finally, five countries do not have specific, targeted programmes for older people. In these cases, poor older people are entitled to the same general social-assistance benefits that are available to the whole population.

Half of OECD countries rely on one primary instrument to prevent old-age poverty, but the rest have a combination of two or three schemes.

2. Second-tier, mandatory, insurance pensions

The second tier in this typology of pension schemes plays an "insurance" role. It aims to ensure that retired people have an adequate replacement rate (retirement income relative to earnings before retirement) and not just a poverty-preventing absolute standard of living. Like the first tier, it is mandatory. Only Ireland and New Zealand do not have some form of mandatory, second-tier provision.

Some 17 countries have public, defined-benefit (DB) plans, making them by far the most common form of pension-insurance provision in OECD countries. In DB schemes, the amount a pensioner will receive depends on the number of years of contributions made throughout the working life and on some measure of individual earnings from work.

The next most common form of pension-insurance provision is the defined-contribution (DC) plan. In these schemes, each worker has an individual account in which contributions are saved and invested, and the accumulated capital is usually converted into a pension-income stream at retirement; lump-sum withdrawals are rarely permitted. Typically, the capital has to be used to buy an annuity, i.e., a guaranteed pension payment until death, which meets certain conditions (such as indexation of benefits and provision of survivors' benefits).

There are different ways in which DC schemes are organised. In Australia, employers must cover their workers through an industry-wide fund or a financial-service company. In Hungary, Mexico and Poland, DC plans are strictly individual: workers choose a pension provider without employer involvement. In Sweden, workers pay only a small contribution into the mandatory individual accounts. They have a wide range of choices of how to invest their savings. A public agency acts as a clearing house and intermediary between workers and investment managers. There is additional DC provision for most workers in Sweden under the quasi-mandatory occupational plans. In Denmark, investments under the national retirement-savings plan are managed centrally, but with choice of portfolio from 2005.

Finally, some countries have earnings-related schemes that do not follow the "traditional" DB model. First, there are points systems: the French occupational plans and the German, Norwegian and Slovak public schemes. Workers earn pension points based on their individual earnings for each year of contributions. At retirement, the sum of pension points is multiplied by a pension-point value to convert them into a regular pension payment.

There are also notional-accounts schemes: the public plans of Italy, Poland and Sweden. These are schemes which record each worker's contributions in an individual account and apply a rate of return to the accounts. The accounts are "notional" in that both the incoming contributions and the interest charged to them exist only on the books of the managing institution. At retirement, the accumulated notional capital in each account is converted into a stream of pension payments using a formula based on life expectancy at the time of retirement.

Mandatory contributions to Swiss occupational plans look at first like a DC scheme, since individuals and their employers must pay a contribution rate that varies with age. But the government sets the minimum rate of return that the scheme must pay and a mandatory annuity rate at which the accumulation is converted into a low of pension payments. This means that the system has strong elements of a DB plan.

Notes

1. Note that Korea is included here because the earnings-related pension scheme has a flat component which pays a percentage of economy-wide average earnings for each year of contributions.

2. Some countries, such as Mexico, call part of their pension system a "minimum pension". But since this is a separate scheme from the second-tier plan, it is here classified as a "targeted" plan.

ISBN 92-64-01871-9
Pensions at a Glance
Public Policies across OECD Countries
© OECD 2005

PART I

Chapter 2

Comparing Pension-system Parameters

The main features of OECD member countries' pension systems are summarised in Table 2.1. This follows the typology of the previous chapter (Table 1.1), dividing the pension system into two tiers. The summary necessarily leaves out much of the institutional details. More complete descriptions are provided in the country studies.

1. First-tier, redistributive schemes

The level of benefits under first-tier, redistributive schemes is expressed as a percentage of average earnings in each country. (Section 4 in Chapter 3 shows the average earnings data and describes their sources.)

In the cases of minimum pensions and basic schemes, the benefit entitlement is shown for a worker who enters at age 20 and works without interruption until he reaches the standard pension eligibility age. In most OECD countries, this is age 65. The social-assistance level is shown only when there is no specific, targeted scheme for poor pensioners. (Only full-career workers with very low earnings will be eligible for the targeted and social-assistance programmes; the majority of beneficiaries will be those with short and interrupted contribution histories.) The final row shows the total, first-tier benefit to which a full-career worker would be entitled. This is relevant because, in some cases, workers can receive several different types of first-tier benefits at the same time, while in others, people are only eligible for one of the different programmes.

The average minimum retirement benefit across OECD countries is a little under 29% of average earnings. The minimum pension in the Czech Republic is exceptionally low at just 12% of average earnings. The basic pension in Japan, minimum pension in Mexico and the targeted scheme in the United States are also on the low side, providing benefits worth one fifth or less of average earnings. At the other end of the spectrum, Luxembourg and Portugal have minimum pensions worth well above 40% of average earnings. Greece's minimum pensions, the targeted plan in Austria and the minimum pension credits in Belgium are also high compared to other OECD countries.

2. Second-tier, earnings-related schemes

The information on the second, earnings-related insurance tier begins with the type of earnings-related scheme that is provided: defined benefit, points or notional accounts. The main parameter which accounts for differences in the value of these schemes is the accrual rate per year of contribution, that is, the rate at which a worker earns benefit entitlements for each year of coverage. The accrual rate is expressed as a percentage of the earnings that are "covered" by the pension scheme. Most pension schemes cover only part of workers' earnings to calculate pension benefits. Often, contributions to the scheme are charged only on part of the earnings. The rationale behind such ceilings is the view that higher-income workers can save individually if they want to reach a high replacement rate.

Only four countries (Australia, Ireland, Mexico and New Zealand) do not have an earnings-related, second-tier scheme. Most countries have schemes of the traditional

Table 2.1. Summary of pension system parameters

	Australia	Austria	Belgium	Canada	Czech Republic	Denmark	Finland	France	Germany	Greece	Hungary	Iceland	Ireland	Italy	Japan
First tier															
(% average earnings)															
Social assistance	–	–	–	–	10	–	–	–	24	–	–	–	–	–	–
Targeted	23	37	23	16	–	17	21	31	–	12	–	25[8]	28	22	–
Basic	–	–	–	14	8	17	–	–	–	–	–	–	31	–	19
Minimum	–	–	38[1]	–	12	–	–	29	–	40	22	–	–	–	–
Overall entitlement	23	37	38	30	12	34	21	31	24	40	22	25	31	22	19
(full-career worker)															
Second tier															
Earnings-related															
Type	None	DB	DB	DB	DB	DB/DC	DB	DB/points	Points	DB	DB	DB	None	N. acs	DB
Accrual rate *(% indiv. earnings)*	–	1.78	1.50	0.63	0.45 [w][2]		1.5 [a][4]	1.75 [w][5,6]	1.00	2.57[5]	1.22	1.40	–		0.71
Defined contribution															
Contribution rate															
(% indiv. earnings)	9	–	–	–	–	1	–	–	–	–	8	–	–	–	–
Ceilings															
(% average earnings)															
Public	–	164	129	100	None	–	–	128	164	325[7]	220	–	–	357	175
Private/occupational	234	–	–	–	–	–	None	385	–	–	220	None	–	–	–
Pension age															
Normal	65	65	65	65	63	65	65	60	65	65	62	67	66	65	65
(women)	–	60			59-63[3]										
Early	55		60	60	60		60		63	57			65	60	60
(women)	–				56-60[3]										

Notes to Table 2.1 (see also country studies, Part II, for fuller details): Parameters are based on 2002 values but include all legislated changes even when these take effect in the future. Pension ages for women are only shown where these are different from those for men. Early pension ages are only shown where relevant.
DB: Defined benefit.
DC: Defined contribution.
N. acs: Notional accounts.
– Not relevant.
[w] = Varies with earnings.
[y] = Varies with years of service.
[a] = Varies with age.

Table 2.1. **Summary of pension system parameters** (cont.)

	Korea	Luxembourg	Mexico	Netherlands	New Zealand	Norway	Poland	Portugal	Slovak Republic	Spain	Sweden	Switzerland	Turkey	United Kingdom	United States
First tier *(% average earnings)*															
Social assistance	–	36	–	–	–	–	–	–	–	–	–	–	–	–	–
Targeted	–	–	19	34	38	33	–	20	–	–	34	26	6	26	20
Basic	30	12	–	34	–	18	–	–	–	–	–	–	–	20	–
Minimum	–	46	–	–	–	–	24	44	*22	33	–	19	28	13[1]	–
Overall entitlement *(full career worker)*	30	46	19	34	38	33	24	44	22	33	34	26	28	33	20
Second tier															
Earnings-related															
Type	DB	DB	None	DB	None	Points	N.acs	DB	Points	DB	N. acs	DB	DB	DB	DB
Accrual rate (% indiv. earnings)	0.75	1.85 [y]⁹	–	1.75[11]	–	1.05 [w][12]	0.67	2.25 [w][2]	1.19	3.0 [y][13]	1.21 [w][5, 6]	[w/a]	2.0 [y][13]	0.89 [w]	0.91 [w][2]
Defined contribution															
Contribution rate (% indiv. earnings)	–	–	6.5[10]	–	–	–	7.3	–	–	–	4.5[5]	–	–	–	–
Ceilings *(% average earnings)*															
Public	189	240[7]	–	–	–	219	245	None	300	189	132	116	173	156	262
Private/occupational	–	–	482	None	–	–	–	–	–	–	367	116	–	–	–
Pension age															
Normal	60	65	65	65	65	67	65	65	62	65	65	65	60	65	67
(women)		–	60				60					64	58		
Early	55	57	–	60		–	–	55		60	61	63	–	–	62
(women)												62			

1. Belgium, United Kingdom: minimum benefit calculated from minimum credit.
2. Czech Republic, Portugal, United States: higher accrual rates for lower earnings, lower accrual rates for higher earnings.
3. Czech Republic: pension ages for women vary with the number of children.
4. Finland: higher accrual rates at older ages.
5. France, Greece, Sweden: data shown combines two different programmes (public and occupational plans).
6. France, Sweden: higher accrual rates for higher earnings.
7. Greece: effective ceiling calculated from maximum pension.
8. Iceland: includes three different programmes (basic pension and two supplements).
9. Luxembourg: accrual rate is higher for longer contribution periods.
10. Mexico: additional contribution of 5.5% of minimum wage.
11. Netherlands: accrual rate varies between occupational schemes.
12. Norway: lower accrual rate for higher earnings.
13. Spain, Turkey: higher accrual rate for early years of service and lower for later years.

Source: Based on information provided by national authorities.

PENSIONS AT A GLANCE – ISBN 92-64-01871-9 – © OECD 2005

defined-benefit variety for which accrual rates can be calculated in a straightforward way. For the alternative types of earnings-related scheme – points systems and notional accounts – it is also possible to calculate an "effective" accrual rate.

For points systems, such as the German public plan, French occupational schemes and the new Slovak public pension, the effective accrual rate shown in Table 2.1 is the ratio of the cost of a pension point to the pension-point value, expressed as percentage of individual earnings. This, like the accrual rate in DB schemes, gives the benefit earned each year as a proportion of earnings in that year. The details of this calculation are set out in Annex I.1.

In the notional-accounts schemes, the effective accrual rate is calculated in a similar way. Again, this ratio gives the annual pension entitlement as a proportion of earnings in a given year. The calculation is again described in detail in Annex I.1.

In a little under half of the countries with earnings-related plans (of all three types), the accrual rates are linear: that is, a single percentage rate applies across the range of covered earnings and to each and every year of coverage. In the other countries, the pension benefit earned for each year of coverage varies, either with individual earnings, with the number of years of contributions or with individual age. Table 2.1 shows a "typical" accrual rate in these cases; the details are provided in the country studies (Part II).

In seven cases, the accrual rate varies with earnings (indicated in Table 2.1 by [w]). In the public schemes of the Czech Republic, Switzerland, Portugal and the United States, the pattern is progressive, giving higher replacement rates to lower-income workers. In the United Kingdom, the accrual rates are U-shaped, highest for low earners, then smaller, then higher again. In the occupational plans of France and Sweden, the schemes are designed to offset the redistribution in the public scheme; they pay a higher replacement rate to high earners on their pay above the ceiling of the public plan.

In the occupational plans of Finland and Switzerland, pension accrual increases with age (shown as [a]).

Three countries have accrual rates that vary with length of service ([y]). In Luxembourg, the accrual rate increases for people with a longer contribution history. In Spain and Turkey, there are three accrual rates. The pattern is the reverse of that in Luxembourg: the highest accrual rate is for the first few years of coverage and the lowest for later years in longer contribution histories.

3. Earnings measures and valorisation in earnings-related schemes

There are two important mechanisms in earnings-related schemes that greatly influence the level of benefits that pensioners will eventually receive. The first is the measure of individual earnings used in the benefit formula. Entitlements in these schemes are calculated in relation to the past earnings of the individual worker but the way in which these are measured differs among countries. The measure might be, for example, a period of final earnings, the lifetime average or a number of best years of earnings. When individual earnings increase over a worker's career, as is often the case, using only final or a few last years of earnings will result in a higher benefit than when taking into account early years of the career when earnings were much lower.

The second mechanism is valorisation, which is often over-looked in pension-policy analysis, but has a large effect on pension entitlements. Past earnings are "valorised" to take account of changes in living standards between the time pension rights accrued and the time

Table 2.2. **Earnings measure and valorisation: earnings-related schemes**

	Measure of individual earnings	Valorisation of earlier years' earnings
Australia	–	–
Austria	Best 15 moving to 40 years	To be decided (average earnings probable)
Belgium	Lifetime average	Prices
Canada	Lifetime average excluding worst 15% of years	Average earnings
Czech Republic	Since 1985 moving to 30 years	Average earnings
Denmark	–	–
Finland	Final 10 years moving to lifetime average	50% prices/average earnings moving to 20%/80%
France	Best 20 moving to 25 years (public) Lifetime average (ARRCO points)	Prices (public) Prices (ARRCO)
Germany	Lifetime average (points)	Average earnings with adjustment for changes in contribution rates and potential contribution to voluntary pensions
Greece	Final 5 years	Increases in pensions of public-sector workers
Hungary	Since 1988 moving to lifetime average	Average earnings
Iceland	Lifetime average (occupational)	Prices
Ireland	–	–
Italy	Lifetime average (notional accounts)	Moving average of nominal GDP growth over 5 years
Japan	Lifetime average	Average earnings
Korea	Lifetime average	Prices
Luxembourg	Lifetime average	Average earnings
Mexico	–	–
Netherlands	Lifetime average for approx. two-thirds and final for one-third of schemes (occupational)	Typically average earnings (occupational)
New Zealand	–	–
Norway	Best 20 years (points)	Average earnings
Poland	Lifetime average (notional accounts)	Prices + 75% of real-wage-bill growth; from 2004, real wage bill growth but at least price inflation
Portugal	Best 10 out of final 15 moving to lifetime average	75% prices and 25% average earnings with maximum real growth of 0.5%
Slovak Republic	Lifetime average (points)	Average earnings
Spain	Final 15 years	Prices up to 2 years before retirement
Sweden	Lifetime average (notional accounts) Final (occupational scheme)	Average earnings with potential adjustment for demographics (notional accounts) No valorisation – final salary
Switzerland	Lifetime average (public scheme) Lifetime average (occupational)	Average earnings Minimum interest rate specified
Turkey	Lifetime average	Nominal GDP growth
United Kingdom	Lifetime average	Average earnings
United States	Best 35 years	Average earnings up to age 60; prices from 62 to 67

– Country does not have an earnings-related scheme.

Source: Based on information provided by national authorities.

they are claimed. In final-salary schemes there is obviously no need for valorisation but it is common in schemes where benefits are based on earnings over a longer period. Both rules are summarised in Table 2.2. Again, more detail is provided in the country studies.

Of the 25 countries with earnings-related schemes, 20 use lifetime average (or close to lifetime average) pay as the earnings measure for calculating pension benefits. This means that all (or nearly all) years of previous earnings count in determining the pension entitlement. The exceptions are the public schemes of France, Greece, Portugal and Spain, the Norwegian points-based scheme and Swedish occupational pensions. Earnings are averaged over shorter periods in these cases. Some countries are currently phasing in longer averaging periods for earnings in their benefit calculation (Austria, Finland, Hungary and Portugal).

Table 2.2 shows valorisation rules – and the equivalent policies for notional accounts and points systems – in the final column.[1] In 14 cases, past earnings are valorised in line with growth of earnings (or close, as in the United States). In Italy and Turkey, adjustments are linked to a measure of GDP growth. Valorisation is purely with prices in Belgium, France (both the public scheme and occupational plans) and Spain. Finland, Poland and Portugal valorise with a mix of earnings and prices.

The effect of valorisation policy on pension entitlements can be very large. This is due to a "compound-interest" effect. On the baseline economic assumptions used in this report – i.e., real wage growth of 2% and price inflation of 2.5% – prices valorisation for a full-career (between age 20 and 65) results in a pension that would be 40% lower than a policy of full adjustment of earlier years' pay in line with economy-wide average earnings.

4. Defined-contribution schemes

Among OECD countries, Australia has the largest mandatory defined contribution scheme: employers must pay 9% of their employees' earnings into their pension accounts. In Mexico, the contribution is 6.5% of earnings with the government paying 5.5% of the minimum wage into all accounts. For an average earner, the total contribution comes to 7.1% of earnings, similar to Poland's contribution rate (7.3%). Hungary has slightly higher contributions (8% of earnings). In Denmark and Sweden, the mandatory contribution rates are much lower. The savings scheme in Denmark requires contributions of just 1% of earnings, but DC occupational plans (which cover the vast majority of employees) have contribution rates that vary between 9 and 17%. In Sweden, where there are two DC programmes, the mandatory scheme requires contributions of 2.5% of earnings and the occupational plan, 2%.

5. Ceilings on pensionable earnings

Most countries do not require high-income workers to contribute to the pension system on their entire earnings. Usually, a limit is set on the earnings used both to calculate contribution liability and pension benefits. This ceiling on the earnings covered by the pension system has an important effect on the structure, size and cost of the second-tier systems. High ceilings or the absence of a ceiling means that high-income workers receive a high replacement rate and there is little need for take-up of voluntary private pensions.

The average ceiling on public pensions for 19 countries is 183% of average economy-wide earnings.[2] In addition to those countries with no ceiling, the ceiling on pensionable pay is very high relative to average pay in Italy. By contrast, at roughly the level of average economy-wide earnings, the Canadian ceiling is exceptionally low. Belgium, France and Sweden also have relatively low ceilings, of the order of 125-135% of average earnings. In these countries, around 15-20% of workers earn above the ceiling of the public scheme.

Table 2.1 also shows ceilings for mandatory private pension systems and for the public, occupational plans in France and Finland. Of the 10 countries with this type of programme, three have no ceiling: Finland, Iceland and the Netherlands. The ceilings of the occupational plans in France and Sweden are three and 2.8 times respectively the cap on pensionable earnings in the public programme (equivalent to well over 3½ times average economy-wide earnings). The ceiling on mandatory contributions to the defined-contribution plan in Mexico is also relatively high, at nearly five times average earnings.

It is possible to calculate an overall ceiling on mandatory pensions, including mandatory private and occupational schemes where appropriate. This averages 225% of average earnings across 21 countries, which is rather higher than the 183% average ceiling on public schemes alone.

6. Pension eligibility ages

Table 2.1 shows that the majority of OECD member countries have a standard retirement age of 65 for men. Pension eligibility ages for women are still lower in several countries but, in most of these, they will be equalised gradually with those of men (Belgium, Hungary and the United Kingdom). Iceland, Norway and the United States stand out as having a standard pension age of 67. At the other extreme, France and Turkey are the only countries which allow normal retirement at age 60. Two-thirds of OECD member countries also have special provisions for early retirement.[3]

7. Indexation of pensions in payment

Indexation refers to the policy for the up-rating of pensions in payment from the point of claim of the pension benefit onwards. Typically, pension benefits are adjusted in line with an index of consumer prices, although in some cases the adjustments also take account of changes in average earnings.

Few countries had formal indexation rules when pension schemes were established. But the high-inflation era of the 1970s led most governments to adopt automatic procedures.[4] There are still a few cases of discretionary adjustments, particularly for social-assistance type benefits or those linked to minimum wages.

However, most indexation is fully to prices. Many countries moved from earnings indexation to prices during the 1980s and 1990s as a cost-cutting measure (given that wages have grown faster than prices in nearly all countries). With price indexation, the purchasing power of pensions is preserved. But the standard of living of individual retirees over time falls behind that of workers.

Some countries, such as Finland, Hungary, Poland and the Slovak Republic have adopted indexation to a mix of price and wage inflation, as pioneered by Switzerland. Table 2.3 gives an overview of procedures for adjusting pensions in payment by both country and pension programme.

8. Taxes and social security contributions

Income taxes and, usually, social security contributions levied on pensioners have an important impact on *net* incomes from pensions relative to earnings during working life.[5] Pensioners often do not pay social security contributions. Personal income taxes are progressive: the average tax rate on (lower) pension income will be less than the tax rate on (higher) earned income since replacement rates are nearly always less than 100%. In addition, most income tax systems give preferential treatment to pensions (exempting some or all of income from tax) or to pensioners (giving additional allowances, credits or zero-rate bands to the elderly). Replacement rates net of taxes and contributions are higher than gross replacement rates.

Table 2.3. **Procedures for adjustment of pensions in payment by country and scheme**

Percentage of total adjustment linked to prices or earnings

	Scheme	Prices	Earnings	Other/notes
Australia	Targeted		100	
	Defined contribution			Individual choice
Austria	Earnings-related			Discretionary; prices assumed in modelling
Belgium	Social assistance	100		
	Minimum pension	100		Price index excludes alcohol, cigarettes and fuel; increases only if inflation
	Earnings-related	100		exceeds 2%
Canada	Targeted	100		
	Basic	100		
	Earnings-related	100		
Czech Republic	Basic	67	33	
	Earnings-related	67	33	Adjustment to prices plus increases of at least one third of real wage
	Minimum	100		growth
Denmark	Targeted		100	
	Basic		100	
	ATP			Discretionary
	Defined contribution			Periodic bonuses
Finland	Basic	100		
	Earnings-related	80	20	
France	Targeted		100	
	Minimum	100		
	Earnings-related	100		
	Occupational	100		No automatic procedure but recent practice
Germany	Social assistance			Discretionary
	Earnings-related		100	Wages net of pension contributions
Greece	Minimum		100	
	Targeted			Discretionary
	Earnings-related			Discretionary
Hungary	Minimum	50	50	
	Earnings-related	50	50	
	Defined contribution	50	50	
Iceland	Targeted		100	In line with public-sector pay
	Occupational	100		Minimum legal uprating
Ireland	Targeted		100	
	Basic pension		100	
Italy	Social assistance			Discretionary
	Earnings-related	75-100		Increase between full and 75% price indexation depending on pension level
Japan	Basic	100		
	Earnings-related	100		
Korea	Earnings-related	100		
Luxembourg	Social assistance			Discretionary
	Basic		100	At least prices with extra increase related to earnings growth
	Minimum		100	
	Earnings-related		100	
Mexico	Minimum	100		Equal to real value of minimum wage for 1997
	Defined contribution	100		Individual can also choose gradual withdrawal
Netherlands	Basic		100	Net minimum wage
	Occupational		100	No legal requirement but customary
New Zealand	Basic		100	
Norway	Targeted		100	
	Basic		100	
	Earnings-related		100	

Table 2.3. **Procedures for adjustment of pensions in payment by country and scheme** (cont.)

Percentage of total adjustment linked to prices or earnings

	Scheme	Prices	Earnings	Other/notes
Poland	Minimum	80	20	
	Defined contribution	100		
Portugal	Targeted			Discretionary increases; recently above prices
	Minimum		100	Minimum wage net of contributions
	Earnings-related	100		
Slovak Republic	Earnings-related	50	50	
Spain	Earnings-related	100		
Sweden	Targeted	100		
	Earnings-related			Gross earnings less "growth norm" of 1.6%
	Occupational		100	
Switzerland	Targeted	50	50	
	Earnings-related	50	50	
	Occupational			Discretionary
Turkey	Targeted	100		
	Earnings-related	100		
United Kingdom	Targeted			Prices or more; up to wages if possible given fiscal situation
	Basic	100		
	Earnings-related	100		
United States	Targeted	100		
	Earnings-related	100		

Source: Based on information provided by national authorities.

The relevant features of personal income taxes and social security contributions are divided into three categories:

- Age-based tax allowances and tax credits, which exceed those available to taxpayers of working age. In many cases, the concessions are targeted on those with modest incomes and are withdrawn as income increases.

- Reliefs for some or all of pension income received. Several countries exempt fully or partially pensions paid from public sources from the personal income tax. And, in some cases, there is a preferential tax treatment for modest pensions paid from private-sector schemes.

- Social security contributions are typically levied only on wage income[6] and not on pension benefits. However, some countries charge contributions on pension income for health and long-term care insurance or for survivors' insurance.

Table 2.4 gives an overview of the three categories of concessions in the 30 OECD countries. Although the table reports concessions to income streams from private pensions, it excludes, for example, reliefs granted to lump-sum withdrawals from personal or occupational pension plans. Furthermore, other aspects of the tax treatment of private pensions (such as the treatment of contributions and investment returns at the fund level) are not considered in this table.

Table 2.4. **Categories of concession available to pensioners**

	Increased tax allowances or tax credit	Relief or partial relief for pension income	Social security contributions paid by pensioners
Australia	✓		–
Austria			Low
Belgium	✓		Low
Canada	✓	✓	None
Czech Republic	✓		None
Denmark		✓	None
Finland	✓		Low
France		✓	Low
Germany		✓	Low
Greece			None
Hungary		✓	None
Iceland			None
Ireland	✓		None
Italy	✓	✓	None
Japan	✓		Low
Korea	✓	✓	None
Luxembourg	✓		Low
Mexico	✓		None
Netherlands	✓		Low
New Zealand			–
Norway	✓	✓	Low
Poland			Low
Portugal			None
Slovak Republic			None
Spain			None
Sweden			None
Switzerland			None
Turkey		✓	None
United Kingdom	✓		None
United States	✓	✓	None

Source: Based on information provided by national authorities.

Notes

1. Adjustments related to valorisation exist also in the different variants of earnings-related schemes. In notional accounts, the exact corollary to valorisation is the notional interest rate applied, which again adjusts benefits between the time they were earned and that time that they are drawn. Similarly, procedures for uprating the value of a pension point in points systems have the same effect. (The detailed reasoning is shown in Annex I.1.)

2. This excludes the eight countries where there is no public pension scheme for which a ceiling is relevant (such as basic or targeted programmes) and the three countries that have no ceiling on earnings eligible for a public pension.

3. Preliminary work on the value of pension benefits at different retirement ages has been published in Casey *et al.* (2003) and OECD (2001).

4. See Weaver (1988). In practice, benefit increases have often strayed from that set out in the rules: see Vordring and Goudswaard (1997).

5. See Whiteford (1995) for a discussion of these issues.

6. There are some social contributions with a broader base than earnings, such as the CSG (*contribution sociale généralisée*) in France.

ISBN 92-64-01871-9
Pensions at a Glance
Public Policies across OECD Countries
© OECD 2005

PART I

Chapter 3

Modelling Pension Entitlements

This report adopts a "microeconomic" approach to comparing retirement-income systems, looking at prospective individual entitlements under all 30 of OECD member countries' pension regimes. These microeconomic techniques were first developed for the retirement-income reviews of nine OECD countries (OECD, 2001).

This chapter outlines the details of the structure, coverage and basic economic and financial assumptions underlying the calculation of future pension entitlements on a comparative basis. It also sets out the main indicators used to compare pensions; these are shown for the 30 OECD countries in Part II.

1. Future entitlements under today's parameters and rules

The pension entitlements that are compared are those that are currently legislated. All pension system parameters reflect the situation in the year 2002.[1] Changes in rules that have already been legislated, but are being phased-in gradually, are assumed to be fully in place from the start.[2] It is assumed that the pension rules remain unchanged.[3, 4]

The calculations show the pension entitlements of a worker who enters the system today and retires after a full career. This is defined here as entering at age 20 and working until the standard pension-eligibility age, which, of course, varies between countries. The implication is that the length of career varies with the statutory retirement age: 40 years for retirement at 60, 45 years for retirement at 65.

The reason for modelling only full careers is that periods out of the labour market are covered in many countries pension systems, with credits for periods in higher education, military service, unemployment, child rearing, etc. Simply assuming that people who are not in work are not covered by the pension system during career gaps would produce inaccurate figures for pension entitlements.

The results are shown for a single person only. This is because the rules governing benefits for married couples are complex in many countries, and because the results depend on assumptions over both partners' career histories.

2. Coverage

The pension models presented here include all *mandatory* pension schemes for private-sector workers, regardless of whether they are public (*i.e.* they involve payments from government or from social security institutions, as defined in the System of National Accounts) or private.[5] Systems with near-universal coverage are also included, provided they cover at least 90% of employees. For example, such a degree of coverage of occupational plans is achieved through centralised collective bargaining in the Netherlands and in Sweden.

In Canada, Denmark, the United Kingdom and the United States, there is broad coverage of voluntary, occupational pensions and these play an important role in providing retirement incomes. However, coverage is significantly below 90%, so they have not been included in the main results. But the results including these schemes are shown as memorandum items in the tables presented in the cross-country analysis below, and the details of the calculations are set out in the country studies.

Mandatory personal pensions, known as "individual accounts" in some countries, are also included. These are of the defined contribution type, so the pension benefit depends on contributions made and investment returns earned. The countries that have recently introduced these schemes have made them mandatory for new labour-market entrants; the majority of older workers are covered only by the old, public scheme in some of these countries.

Resource-tested benefits for which retired people may be eligible are also included. As described above, these can be means-tested, where both assets and income are taken into account, purely income-tested or withdrawn only against pension income. Leaving these benefits out of the model would give a misleading picture of the situation of low-income retirees. The comparisons assume all entitled pensioners take up these benefits.[6] Where there are broader means tests, taking account also of assets, the income test is taken as binding. It is assumed that the whole of income during retirement comes from the mandatory pension scheme when calculating pensions entitlements (or from the voluntary pension in the four countries where these are modelled).

In some OECD countries there are entirely separate schemes for civil servants and other public-sector workers.[7] Some also have special programmes for agricultural workers and the self-employed. These are not included here. The comparisons currently look only at the main national scheme for private-sector employees.

Pension entitlements are compared for workers with earnings between 0.3 times and three times the economy-wide average. This large range permits the pensions of both the poorest and richer workers to be examined, and it is sufficiently broad to include people who are employed part-time.

3. Economic variables

The comparisons are based upon a single set of economic assumptions for all 30 countries. In practice, the level of pensions received is affected by economic growth, wage growth and inflation, and these will vary across countries. A single set of assumptions, however, ensures that the outcomes of the different pension regimes are not affected by different economic conditions. In this way, differences across countries in pension levels reflect differences in pension systems and policies alone.

The baseline assumptions are:

- real earnings growth: 2% per year (given the assumption for price inflation, this implies nominal wage growth of 4.55%);
- individual earnings: assumed to grow in line with the economy-wide average. This means that, in the baseline case, the individual is assumed to remain at the same point in the earnings distribution, earning the same percentage of average earnings in every year of the working life;
- price inflation: 2.5% per year;
- real rate of return on funded, defined-contribution pensions: 3.5% per year;
- discount rate (for actuarial calculations): 2% per year;

- mortality rates: the baseline modelling uses country-specific projections (made in 2002) from the United Nations/World Bank population database for the year 2040;

- earnings distribution: composite indicators use the OECD average earnings distribution (based on 16 countries) with country-specific data used where available.

Changes in these baseline assumptions will obviously affect the resulting pension entitlements. A sensitivity analysis of the effect of these assumptions is presented in Annex I.2. This analysis allows, for example, for economy-wide earnings growth of between zero and 3% per year, for returns on defined-contribution schemes of between zero and 6% per year and for individual earnings that grow faster than the economy-wide average by up to two percentage points per year or slower by up to one percentage point per year.

The real rate of return on defined-contribution pensions is assumed to be net of administrative charges. In practice, this assumption might disguise genuine differences in administrative fees between countries.[8]

The calculations assume the following for the pay-out of pension benefits: when DC benefits are received upon retirement, they are paid in the form of a price-indexed life annuity at an actuarially-fair price.[9] This is calculated from mortality data. Because of improvements in life expectancy, someone retiring at a given age after having contributed a given amount to a DC scheme will in the future receive a lower pension than a person retiring today would receive. Similarly, the notional annuity rate in notional accounts schemes is calculated from mortality data using the indexation rules and discounting assumptions employed by the respective country.

4. Average earnings data

It is difficult to produce data on average earnings that are consistent across countries. Consequently, the OECD's average production worker series is currently the only one available for all 30 member countries. The series shows average earnings for full-time adult workers in manufacturing.[10] The data for 2002 are shown in Table 3.1. For comparison across countries, earnings are also shown in US dollars. The conversions are calculated using the average market exchange rate for 2002 and the exchange rate calculated using purchasing power parities (that is, the exchange rate that equalises the cost of a standard basket of goods and services between countries).

5. Taxes and social security contributions

The information on taxes and social security contributions on which the calculations of the net indicators are based can be found in each country study (Part II). The studies describe the tax and social security contribution regimes in each country as they applied to pensioners in 2002.[11] General provisions and the tax treatment of workers for 2002 can be found in the OECD report *Taxing Wages* (2003). The conventions used in that report, such as which payments are considered taxes, are followed here.

6. Indicators and results

The basic indicators used in this report are:

- the *replacement rate*: pension entitlements as a share of individual lifetime average earnings;

- the *relative pension level*: pension entitlements as a share of average economy-wide earnings; and

- *pension wealth*: the discounted stream of future pension payments.

Table 3.1. **Earnings of the average production worker, 2002**

National currency and USD at market and purchasing-power-parity exchange rates

	Earnings of average production worker			Exchange rates with USD	
	National currency	USD, market	USD, PPPs	Market	PPPs
Australia	48 568	26 377	35 727	1.84	1.36
Austria	23 881	22 506	25 840	1.06	0.92
Belgium	30 629	28 865	33 739	1.06	0.91
Canada	38 867	24 756	32 521	1.57	1.20
Czech Republic	206 412	6 306	14 542	32.73	14.19
Denmark	304 925	38 675	35 915	7.88	8.49
Finland	27 682	26 088	27 947	1.06	0.99
France	21 978	20 712	23 766	1.06	0.92
Germany	32 902	31 007	34 252	1.06	0.96
Greece	11 395	10 739	15 144	1.06	0.75
Hungary	1 077 816	4 187	9 279	257.45	116.16
Iceland	2 567 086	28 028	27 053	91.59	94.89
Ireland	25 477	24 010	24 864	1.06	1.02
Italy	21 408	20 175	26 337	1.06	0.81
Japan	4 254 270	33 966	29 012	125.25	146.64
Korea	22 885 416	18 293	31 299	1 251.05	731.18
Luxembourg	31 358	29 552	31 671	1.06	0.99
Mexico	59 702	6 180	9 123	9.66	6.54
Netherlands	30 575	28 814	32 561	1.06	0.94
New Zealand	39 912	18 450	27 118	2.16	1.47
Norway	292 200	36 591	32 183	7.99	9.08
Poland	26 352	6 456	13 905	4.08	1.90
Portugal	8 410	7 926	12 093	1.06	0.70
Slovak Republic	137 316	3 031	8 819	45.30	15.57
Spain	16 360	15 418	21 214	1.06	0.77
Sweden	237 820	24 465	24 076	9.72	9.88
Switzerland	64 169	41 219	33 128	1.56	1.94
Turkey	9 938 274 440	6 571	14 977	1 512 342.00	663 575.48
United Kingdom	19 420	29 133	30 091	0.67	0.65
United States	32 360	32 360	32 360	1.00	1.00

PPP: Purchasing Power Parities.

Source: Earnings data from OECD (2003), *Taxing Wages*, OECD, Paris. Exchange rates are averages for 2002 from IMF database.

The *replacement rate* can be interpreted as an indicator of the *insurance* role of a pension system, since it shows to what extent pension systems aim to preserve the previous, personal standard of living of a worker moving from employment into retirement. Often, the replacement rate is expressed as the ratio of the pension over the final earnings a worker had before retirement. However, the indicator used here shows the pension benefit as a share of *individual lifetime average earnings* (revalued in line with economy-wide earnings growth). Under the baseline assumptions, workers earn the same percentage of economy-wide average earnings throughout their career, meaning that their individual earnings track the assumed growth in economy-wide earnings. In this case, lifetime average revalued earnings and individual final earnings are identical.[12] If people move up the earnings distribution as they get older, then their earnings just before retirement will be higher than they were on average over their lifetime. In that case, replacement rates calculated on individual final earnings will be lower than when calculated on the basis of individual lifetime average revalued earnings. The sensitivity analysis in Annex I.2 illustrates the effects of different individual career earnings profiles on pension entitlements in several countries.

Box 3.1. **Modelling pensions**

X starts working at age 20 and works continuously until he retires at age 65. He starts out with an annual salary of USD 10 000. This corresponds to 75% of economy-wide average earnings at that time. His earnings grow by 2% each year. Economy-wide earnings grow at the same rate. X thus earns 75% of average earnings over his entire career.

When X retires, all his past salaries are increased in line with the growth in economy-wide average earnings between the time that they were earned and the retirement age. The procedure of adjusting past salaries is called "valorization" in this report. In this case, valorisation is linked to economy-wide average earnings growth. X's lifetime average revalued salary, which is the earnings measure used in the pension calculation, is USD 23 900.

The explanation is as follows. Taking i as the number of years since labour-market entry, valorisation means that each year's earnings are increased by $1.02^{(44-i)}$. Each year, X's earnings increase by a constant amount, so at any given time, they are equal to earnings at entry age (USD 10 000) multiplied by 1.02^i. So, in each and every year of the working life, revalued earnings are first-year earnings multiplied by $1.02^{44-I} \times 1.02^i$, giving average lifetime revalued earnings of USD 10 000 $\times 1.02^{44}$ = USD 23 900.

The pension system has an accrual rate of 1.5% of earnings per year. X's gross pension is thus $45 \times 0.015 \times$ USD 23 900 = USD 16 130. His **gross replacement rate** is USD 16 130/ USD 23 900 = 67.5%.

On his gross pension, X has to pay 10% in taxes and health insurance contributions. The net pension is therefore USD 16 130 $\times$ (100 – 10)% = USD 14 510. While he was working, X had to pay 20% in taxes and social security contributions, meaning that his net earnings at the time of retirement were USD 19 120. His **net replacement rate** is therefore USD 14 510/USD 19 120 = 75.9%.

To assess his pension level relative to average earnings, X divides his gross pension entitlement by gross average economy-wide earnings in the year of retirement. X's earnings at retirement are USD 23 900, while the economy wide average is USD 31 790 (since X earns 75% of the average). Thus, X's **gross relative pension level** is USD 16 130/USD 31 790 = 50.8%.

The net relative pension level is calculated in the same way but using the taxes and social security contributions that X pays as a pensioner and those paid by a worker on average gross earnings. Workers on average gross earnings pay 25% in taxes and social security contributions, giving net average earnings of USD 31 790 $\times$ (100 – 25)% = USD 24 840. Therefore, X's **net relative pension level** is USD 14 510/USD 24 840 = 60.9%.

When X retires, male life expectancy at age 65 will be 83 years in his country, giving an expected retirement duration of 18 years. X's pension wealth is the discounted stream of pension payments during retirement, weighted by the probability that he will still be alive at that particular age. The discount rate is designed to reflect the fact that money received in the future is worth less than money received today; the rate used is 2% per year. The calculation also allows for the post-retirement adjustment of pension benefits: in this case, X's pension is increased annually in line with price inflation. The actuarial calculations show that the present value of pension benefits is 14.8 times the annual flow (which is less than the 18 years expected duration of retirement because future benefits are discounted). His **gross pension wealth** is thus USD 16 130 $\times$ 14.8 = USD 238 720. Usually, this is expressed as a multiple of economy-wide average earnings, giving gross pension wealth of USD 238 720/ USD 31 790 = 7.5. **Net pension wealth** is calculated in a similar way.

The *relative pension level* is best seen as an indicator of pension *adequacy*, since it shows what benefit level a pensioner will receive in relation to the average wage earner in the respective country. Individual replacement rates may be quite high, but the pensioner may still receive only a small fraction of economy-wide average earnings. If, for example, a low-income worker – who earned only 30% of economy-wide average earnings – has a replacement rate of 100%, the benefit will only amount to 30% of economy-wide average earnings. For an average-wage earner, the replacement rate and the relative pension level will be the same.

To compare countries which use different earnings measures, pension entitlements for all countries are presented as a proportion of individual lifetime average earnings revalued in line with growth in economy-wide average earnings. Most OECD earnings-related pension schemes use individual lifetime average pay revalued in line with economy-wide average earnings – the exact same – as the earnings measure to calculate pensions (Table 2.2). However, for a few countries, the replacement rates presented here look different from those calculated using the earnings measure from the rules of the national pension systems.

Pension wealth is an indicator that takes into account all future pension payments to a retiree. It therefore depends not only on the level of pensions paid, but also how long they are paid for. The number of years that someone can expect to receive a pension will depend both on the age of retirement and life expectancy at that age (see Box 3.1). The way that benefits are adjusted to price and/or wage growth during the period of payment will also influence pension wealth. The details of calculating pension wealth are set out in Chapter 6.

Notes

1. This year was chosen because it was the latest year for which the OECD tax models were available.

2. In some cases where there has been systemic change, such as in the Slovak Republic and Sweden, the modelling calculates what the parameters of the new system would have been had it been in place in 2002. This ensures that tax rules and average earnings data are the right match for the parameter values. In a few other cases, such as France and the United Kingdom, structural reforms were included even though they were legislated after 2002.

3. McHale (1999) studies the impact of reforms on future pension entitlements in the G7 countries. Diamond (1997) argues that pension systems can be excessively responsive to short-term fiscal conditions (given the limited ability of the elderly to absorb these changes).

4. This "steady-state" assumption is also applied to "value" parameters, such as the level of ceilings or basic pensions. These are assumed to remain at the same level relative to average earnings.

5. It is, of course, possible to separate out the different components of the pension package and look at public pensions alone. The charts in the country studies and Table 7.2 in Chapter 7 show the contribution to total pension benefits made by different parts of the package.

6. People might not claim a benefit to which they are entitled for a number of reasons, including ignorance of entitlement, stigma, and administrative "hassle". These are unlikely to apply to basic or earnings-related public pensions. However, the situation can be different for resource-tested old-age pensions, including social assistance and minimum pension guarantees. There is, for example, evidence from the United Kingdom that take-up can be lower than 70% (see Department of Work and Pensions, 2003). See also Hernanz, Malherbert and Pellizzari (2004).

7. See Palacios and Whitehouse (2005) for a survey of pension provision for public-sector workers.

8. See Whitehouse (2000) and Whitehouse (2001).

9. Studies of voluntary annuity markets in the United Kingdom and the United States have shown that annuities pay out less than they would if insurance companies were to base their calculations on the relevant interest rates and projected population mortality. This does not mean that prices are "actuarially unfair" since they reflect the longer life expectancy of people who choose to buy an annuity. In mandatory annuity markets, which are relevant to the mandatory DC schemes modelled in this report, prices are much closer to the actuarially fair level (Finkelstein and Poterba, 2002, 2004).

10. OECD (2005) contains a special feature on the relationship between earnings of the average production worker on the OECD definition and averages of earnings calculated across broader groups of workers.

11. The modelling assumes that tax systems and social-security contributions remain unchanged in the future. This implicitly means that "value" parameters, such as tax allowances or contribution ceilings, are adjusted annually in line with average earnings, while "rate" parameters, such as the personal income tax schedule and social security contribution rates, remain unchanged.

12. Individual earnings in any time period i can be expressed as a multiple of earnings in the base period (w0): $w_i = w_0 (1 + g)^i$, where w is earnings and g is the growth of (individual and economy-wide) earnings. Revaluing pay in line with earnings growth gives for each period: $w_i = w_0 (1 + g)^i (1 + g)^{R - i}$. This is constant over time and so final and lifetime average revalued earnings are equal in this case.

ISBN 92-64-01871-9
Pensions at a Glance
Public Policies across OECD Countries
© OECD 2005

PART I

Chapter 4

Replacement Rates

This chapter shows gross and net pension replacement rates for the 30 OECD countries. For each country replacement rates are shown for people with different levels of earnings. Detailed results are shown in the country studies.

1. Gross replacement rates

Table 4.1 shows gross replacement rates by level of individual earnings for all countries. Figure 4.1 summarises the information for low, average and high earners, defined as workers earning half, once and twice average earnings, respectively.

The replacement rate at average earnings is perhaps the most familiar indicator in pension analysis. At this earnings level, the OECD average gross replacement rate is 57%, with substantial variation between member countries. Luxembourg is an outlier: the replacement rate for a full-career worker exceeds 100% (meaning that the pension is higher than earnings before retirement). Austria, Greece, Hungary, Italy, Spain and Turkey also provide generous pensions to full-career workers on average earnings: replacement rates exceed 75%. The gross replacement rate at average earnings is around 50% in France, Iceland, Japan, Norway and the Slovak Republic. Not surprisingly, Ireland – which has only basic and targeted pensions and no earnings-related scheme – has the lowest replacement rate at average earnings. In Mexico, the average earner receives only a pension from the defined-contribution scheme. The contribution rate to this plan is fairly low so eventual pensions are also low. Contribution rates in Australia, Hungary and Poland are somewhat higher. The last two countries also top up the defined-contribution pension with a public, earnings-related pension payment. In the United Kingdom, the earnings-related public scheme does not result in a high pension: it has a low accrual rate and does not cover the first slice of earnings (up to around one fifth of the average).[1]

At low earnings, defined as half of the average, the pension entitlements of full-career workers vary less than they do at average earnings. Again, Luxembourg has the highest pensions, offering a replacement rate above 115%. But apart from Luxembourg and Turkey, another set of countries can be categorised as providing a relatively high pension to low-income workers while replacement rates were not to so high at average earnings. Portugal pays a higher accrual rate to low-income workers in its public scheme. Sweden has a relatively high income-tested pension.

The countries at the bottom of the scale are those with the lowest first-tier pensions. German social assistance, Mexican and Polish minimum pensions, the minimum credit in the Slovak Republic and the means-tested scheme in the United States all pay around one fifth of average economy-wide earnings. Countries with redistributive systems, such as Canada, New Zealand and the United Kingdom, pay little to workers on average earnings but they move more towards the middle of the scale when it comes to benefits for low earners. Dutch pensions appear to be relatively low for low earners (compared with the position of middle earners) despite the fact that the basic pension, worth more than a third of average earnings, is at a fairly high level. This is because of the "franchise", a calculation

Table 4.1. **Gross replacement rates by earnings level, mandatory pension programmes, men**

Per cent of individual pre-retirement gross earnings

	Individual earnings, multiple of average					
	0.5	0.75	1	1.5	2	2.5
Australia	65.1	48.4	40.0	31.7	26.2	21.9
Austria	78.3	78.3	78.3	78.3	64.3	51.5
Belgium	61.6	41.1	40.7	34.9	26.2	20.9
Canada	72.4	52.4	42.5	28.4	21.3	17.0
Czech Republic	70.5	53.3	44.4	31.7	25.4	21.6
Denmark	82.4	56.4	43.3	30.3	23.8	19.8
Finland	80.0	71.5	71.5	71.5	71.5	71.5
France	84.2	56.1	52.9	50.7	47.4	45.4
Germany	47.3	45.8	45.8	45.8	37.6	30.1
Greece	84.0	84.0	84.0	84.0	84.0	84.0
Hungary	75.4	75.4	75.4	75.4	75.4	66.3
Iceland	85.5	63.7	52.8	42.8	41.3	40.3
Ireland	61.3	40.9	30.6	20.4	15.3	12.3
Italy	78.8	78.8	78.8	78.8	78.8	78.8
Japan	69.2	56.6	50.3	44.0	36.9	29.5
Korea	60.9	47.4	40.6	33.8	29.3	23.5
Luxembourg	115.5	106.5	101.9	97.4	95.2	89.8
Mexico	39.1	37.0	36.0	34.9	34.4	34.1
Netherlands	68.7	68.3	68.3	68.3	68.3	68.3
New Zealand	75.1	50.1	37.6	25.0	18.8	15.0
Norway	65.3	56.1	52.6	46.5	38.4	31.8
Poland	56.9	56.9	56.9	56.9	56.9	55.8
Portugal	103.1	68.8	66.7	65.9	65.5	64.7
Slovak Republic	48.6	48.6	48.6	48.6	48.6	48.6
Spain	81.2	81.2	81.2	81.2	76.7	61.3
Sweden	87.8	72.5	64.8	64.6	66.2	67.1
Switzerland	62.8	60.2	58.2	44.2	33.1	26.5
Turkey	96.2	90.2	87.2	84.1	71.9	57.5
United Kingdom	67.4	46.4	37.1	29.3	22.5	18.0
United States	49.6	42.3	38.6	33.2	28.1	25.1
OECD average	**72.5**	**61.2**	**56.9**	**52.1**	**47.6**	**43.3**
With voluntary schemes						
Canada	88.2	74.8	70.3	63.1	59.4	57.3
Denmark	113.3	85.0	70.8	56.6	51.1	48.9
United Kingdom	78.8	65.4	58.7	52.0	48.7	46.7
United States	90.4	81.9	77.7	73.4	67.9	64.3
Women, where different						
Austria	74.0	69.4	69.4	69.4	57.0	45.6
Mexico	38.8	25.9	21.7	21.1	20.7	20.5
Poland	48.4	41.4	41.4	41.4	41.4	40.6
Switzerland	63.0	60.7	58.8	44.7	33.5	26.8
Turkey	94.2	88.2	85.2	82.2	70.2	56.2

Source: OECD pension models.

mechanism applied in the Netherlands, which cuts occupational pension entitlements by the value of the basic pension received. At half-average earnings, the occupational benefit is zero as a result of this practice.

Figure 4.1. **Gross replacement rates at different earnings levels**
Percentage of individual pre-retirement earnings

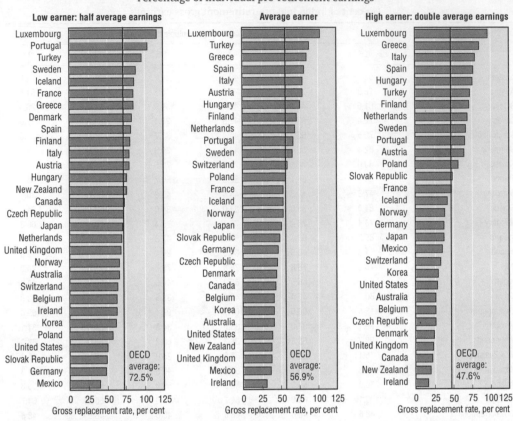

Source: OECD pension models.

Finally, at high earnings (double the average), Luxembourg is yet again an outlier, although the replacement rate at this earnings level is a little short of 100%. It is followed by Greece and Italy, due to the very high ceilings on pensionable earnings in both countries. The other top slots are taken by the same countries that paid the highest pensions to average earners. The rankings mainly reflect the effect of ceilings; these are less than twice average earnings in Turkey and Hungary.

The countries with pure flat-rate systems – Ireland and New Zealand – are naturally the least generous to these high earners, even with New Zealand's exceptionally high basic pension of nearly 40% of average earnings. Canada and the United Kingdom – although they have earnings-related schemes – also provide benefits that are broadly flat-rate (see below).

Table 4.1 also shows replacement rates at different levels of earnings in voluntary, occupational pension schemes for four countries where these play a significant role. Unsurprisingly, these four countries all have mandatory pension provision towards the bottom of the scale, particularly for average and high earners. Including benefits from these voluntary schemes, replacement rates in the United Kingdom are a little higher than the OECD average across the earnings range while in Canada and the United States, the difference is significantly larger. In Denmark, pension entitlements are very high – on a par even with Luxembourg – for low earners and very generous higher up the earnings range once voluntary pensions are taken into account.[2]

Finally, Table 4.1 presents pension replacement rates for women in the five countries where these differ from those of men (due to a lower pension eligibility age for women than for men). The difference between the sexes in replacement rates is particularly stark in the two countries with defined-contribution schemes: Mexico and Poland. In both countries, normal pension age for women is 60 while for men it is 65. This means that women accumulate capital in the individual pension accounts over a shorter period. It also means that women spend a longer period in retirement over which pension capital must be spread. As a result, replacement rates at average earnings are around one third smaller for women than they are for men. The same effect arises in Poland's notional-accounts scheme.

In Switzerland and Turkey, the difference in replacement rates between the sexes is much smaller because the difference in eligibility age is one and two years respectively (compared with five years for Mexico and Poland). In both cases the accrual rates vary. In Turkey, this favours early years of contributions over later years, reducing the difference between pension entitlements even though there is a difference in eligibility age. In Switzerland, the system is designed in a way that women receive a higher accrual than men at certain ages under the mandatory occupational scheme.

2. Net replacement rates

Figure 4.2 and Table 4.2 show net replacement rates: that is, individual net pensions relative to individual net earnings, taking account of personal income taxes and social

Figure 4.2. **Net replacement rates at different earnings levels**

Percentage of individual pre-retirement earnings

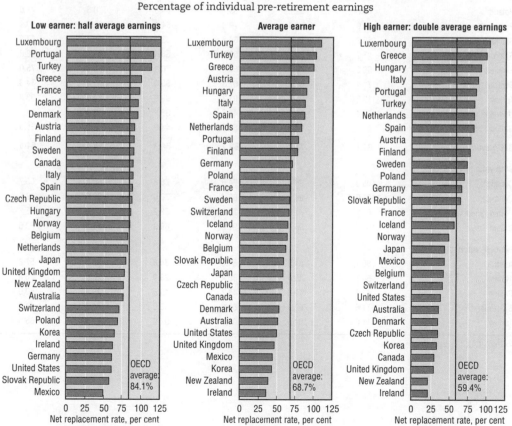

Source: OECD pension models.

Table 4.2. **Net replacement rates by earnings level, mandatory pension programmes, men**

Per cent of individual pre-retirement net earnings

	Individual earnings, multiple of average					
	0.5	0.75	1	1.5	2	2.5
Australia	77.0	61.2	52.4	43.1	36.5	31.3
Austria	91.2	93.4	93.2	93.5	79.3	63.2
Belgium	82.7	63.8	63.1	53.3	42.7	36.0
Canada	89.4	67.6	57.1	39.5	30.6	25.1
Czech Republic	88.3	68.3	58.2	42.9	35.3	31.0
Denmark	95.6	68.0	54.1	42.5	35.5	30.8
Finland	90.7	78.8	78.8	79.2	78.3	79.3
France	98.0	70.8	68.8	62.6	59.2	57.0
Germany	61.7	66.6	71.8	79.2	67.0	54.2
Greece	99.9	99.9	99.9	99.9	99.9	99.9
Hungary	86.6	90.9	90.5	99.1	92.6	81.8
Iceland	95.8	77.1	65.9	54.1	57.2	55.1
Ireland	63.0	47.0	36.6	27.4	21.9	18.3
Italy	89.3	88.0	88.8	88.4	89.1	89.0
Japan	80.1	66.3	59.1	51.9	44.3	35.8
Korea	65.3	51.4	44.3	38.1	34.0	27.8
Luxembourg	125.0	115.0	109.8	105.6	104.2	100.1
Mexico	50.4	46.4	45.1	44.3	44.1	44.2
Netherlands	82.5	88.2	84.1	85.8	83.8	82.8
New Zealand	77.1	52.0	39.5	27.9	22.0	18.1
Norway	85.5	73.1	65.1	58.2	50.1	42.8
Poland	69.6	69.7	69.7	69.8	70.5	71.0
Portugal	115.9	79.8	79.8	84.4	86.3	86.9
Slovak Republic	58.2	59.4	60.2	63.1	65.7	67.8
Spain	88.7	89.4	88.3	88.4	83.4	68.8
Sweden	90.2	76.4	68.2	70.1	74.3	75.0
Switzerland	71.4	68.9	67.3	53.0	41.4	34.3
Turkey	113.2	106.7	103.3	99.9	84.3	66.8
United Kingdom	78.4	57.7	47.6	38.2	29.8	24.7
United States	61.4	54.6	51.0	44.9	39.0	35.5
OECD average	**84.1**	**73.2**	**68.7**	**64.3**	**59.4**	**54.5**
With voluntary schemes						
Canada	108.9	96.4	94.6	78.8	68.8	63.7
Denmark	125.0	96.9	82.4	72.5	66.6	62.8
United Kingdom	90.3	77.5	70.1	62.2	57.5	55.7
United States	105.7	96.1	91.9	89.3	84.2	80.6
Women, where different						
Austria	86.1	84.8	84.6	84.6	72.5	57.8
Mexico	50.1	35.4	30.4	28.9	28.5	28.4
Poland	62.1	49.0	48.7	48.5	48.8	50.0
Switzerland	71.6	69.5	68.0	53.6	41.8	34.7
Turkey	111.0	104.5	101.1	97.8	82.4	65.4

Source: OECD pension models.

security contributions paid by workers and pensioners. The calculations are again carried out for individuals at different levels of gross earnings.

At average earnings, net replacement rates across the 30 OECD countries are, on average, 22% higher than gross replacement rates. The pattern of replacement rates across countries is also different on a net rather than a gross basis. The Belgian, French and German pension systems have higher net replacement rates than gross because of favourable treatment of pension income or pensioners under the personal income tax or social security contributions. In contrast, Korea moves lower down the chart on a net basis. This is because the low general level of direct taxation in Korea means that gross and net replacement rates are much closer together than they are in countries with a larger tax burden, such as most European countries.

The effect of taxes and contributions on net replacement rates for low earners (at half average earnings) is more muted. This is because low-income workers typically pay less in taxes and contributions than those on average earnings. In many cases, their retirement incomes are below the level of income-tax standard reliefs (allowances, credits, etc.). Thus, they are unable to benefit fully from these reliefs. Compared with the 22% differential between net and gross replacement rates at average earnings, the difference for low earners is about 17% on average. Belgium, Canada, the Czech Republic and Norway have much higher replacement rates for low earners measure on a net basis. The reverse is true in France, New Zealand, Sweden and the United Kingdom.

For high earners, personal income taxes and social security contributions play a greater role than for average earners: the differential between net and gross replacement rates is 27% compared with 22% at average pay. The tax system therefore reduces the progressivity of retirement-income systems.

Notes

1. In most of the countries with modest public schemes voluntary pensions are important. For the effects of voluntary pensions on replacement rates see below.

2. A full description of voluntary pension schemes and how they are modelled can be found in the country studies.

ISBN 92-64-01871-9
Pensions at a Glance
Public Policies across OECD Countries
© OECD 2005

PART I

Chapter 5

Relative Pension Levels

The relative pension level is the individual pension divided by economy-wide average earnings, rather than by individual earnings as in the replacement-rate results in the previous chapter. Figure 5.1 shows relative pension levels in OECD member countries on the vertical axis and individual pre-retirement earnings on the horizontal. Countries have been grouped by the degree to which pension benefits are related (or not) to individual pre-retirement earnings.*

In the first set of seven countries (Figures 5.1A and 5.1B), there is little or no link between pension entitlements and pre-retirement earnings. In Ireland and New Zealand, pension benefits are purely flat rate. In Canada, the relative pension level varies little: from 36% for low earners to 42% for those on average earnings and above. Although Canada has an earnings-related pension scheme, its target replacement rate is very low, its ceiling is set at average economy-wide earnings and a resource-tested benefit is withdrawn against additional income from the earnings-related scheme. Thus, the relative pension level changes little with individual pre-retirement earnings although the composition of the pension package varies (between targeted, basic and earnings-related benefits). In Denmark, basic and targeted schemes dominate the mandatory retirement-income regime.

In the Czech Republic and the United Kingdom, the earnings-related schemes have strongly progressive formulae; both countries also have basic pension programmes. The result, again, is a curve of relative pension level against individual earnings that is almost flat. In Australia, the relatively flat curve results mainly from the means-tested public pension programme. There is also a limit to the earnings for which employers must contribute to the DC scheme and the tax system reduces the amount going into DC plans for higher-income workers.

At the other end of the spectrum lie six countries with a very strong link between pension entitlements and pre-retirement earnings (Figure 5.1F) and eight countries with a strong link (Figure 5.1E). In the Netherlands, there is no ceiling to pensionable earnings in the quasi-mandatory occupational schemes. In the Slovak Republic and Italy, ceilings on pensionable earnings are set at three times or more average economy-wide earnings. For low-paid workers, top-ups from the minimum pensions in the Slovak Republic and Poland and the basic pension in the Netherlands are apparent in the charts. But apart from this narrow earnings range (and the impact of the ceilings in Hungary and Poland), relative pension levels increase with individual earnings in a linear way. The contrast with the seven countries in Figures 5.1A and 5.1B – where pension values were constant or close to flat and so replacement rates decline with earnings – is stark.

The eight countries in Figure 5.1E have a slightly weaker link between individual pre-retirement earnings and pensions than those in Figure 5.1F. There are two main explanations. First, Austria, Luxembourg, Spain and Sweden have redistributive programmes

---

* Categorisation is based on the value of the Gini coefficient of the distribution of pension levels across the earnings range weighted by the OECD average distribution of earnings. The calculation method and results are set out in Annex I.3 on progressivity of pension benefit formulae.

Figure 5.1. **The link between pre-retirement earnings and pension entitlements**

Gross pension entitlement as a proportion of economy-wide average earnings

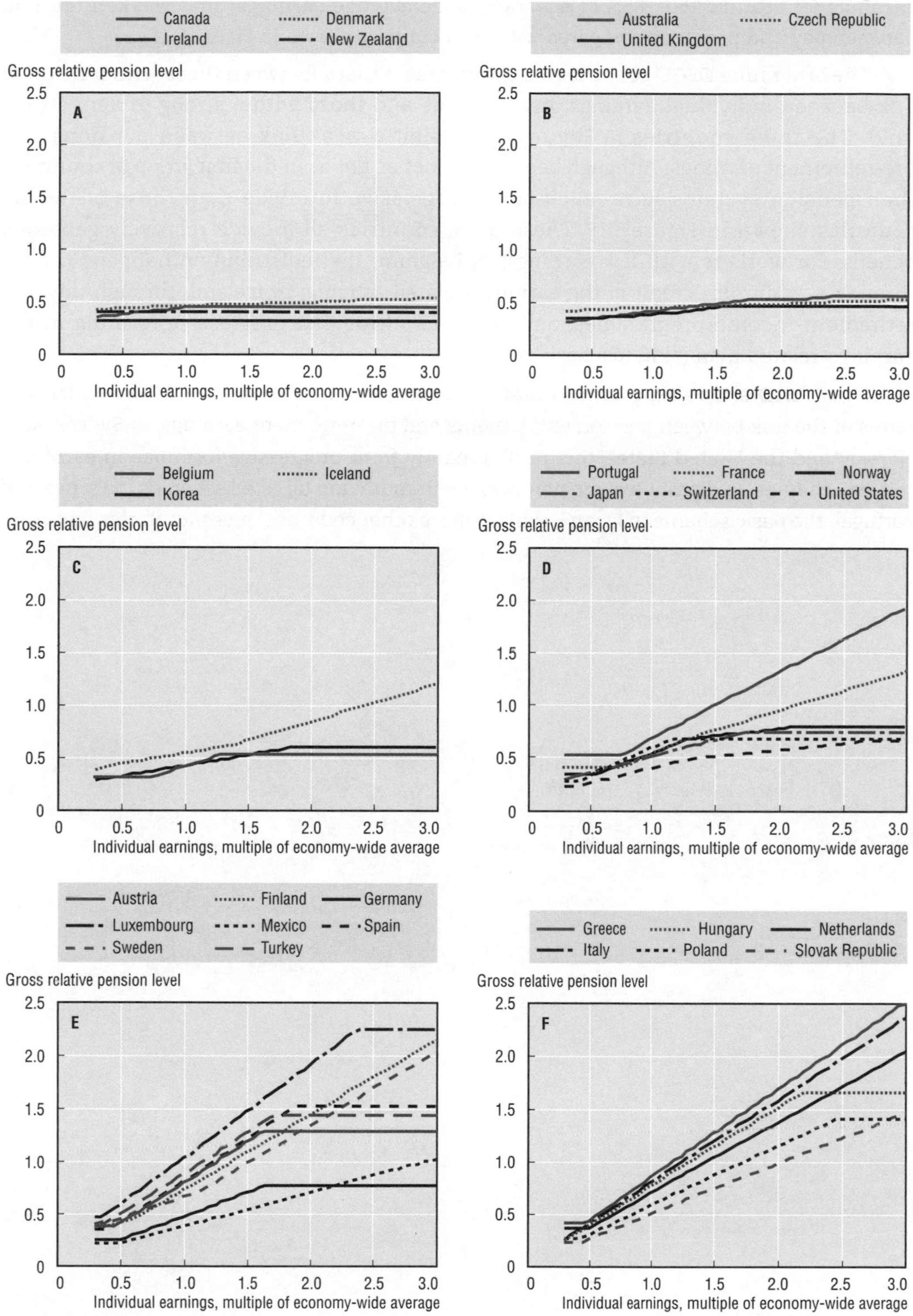

Source: OECD pension models.

targeting a relatively high minimum income (of around one third of economy-wide average earnings). Secondly, Austria, Germany, Spain and Turkey have ceilings to pensionable earnings (of around 160-185% of economy-wide average earnings) that weaken the link between pay and pensions compared with the countries shown in Figure 5.1F.

The other nine OECD countries are intermediate cases (between those with little or no link between individual earnings and pensions and those with a strong or very strong link). The three countries in Figure 5.1C exhibit a weak link between pensions and pre-retirement earnings. Although benefits are not as flat as in the first group of countries, their pension systems have much more progressive formulae than those of the six countries shown in Figure 5.1F. These three countries all provide relatively generous benefits for workers with low earnings. In Belgium, the redistribution happens mainly through a minimum credit in the earnings-related scheme; in Iceland, through targeted retirement-income programmes; and, in Korea, through a progressive formula in the earnings-related plan (akin to a basic scheme).

Figure 5.1D shows six countries that lie towards the middle of the OECD countries in terms of the link between pension entitlements and pre-retirement earnings. In Switzerland, Norway and the United States, this results mainly from progressive formulae in earnings-related schemes. Redistributive programmes – minimum and targeted schemes in France and Portugal, the basic scheme in Japan – explain these other countries' presence in this group.

ISBN 92-64-01871-9
Pensions at a Glance
Public Policies across OECD Countries
© OECD 2005

PART I

Chapter 6

Pension Wealth

The replacement rates and relative pension levels discussed above give a first indication of the magnitude of the pension promise, but they are not comprehensive measures. For a full picture, it is necessary to take account of life expectancy, retirement ages and the indexation of pension benefits. These determine for how long the pension benefit must be paid and how its value evolves over time. To compare countries' different provisions, the pension entitlement at retirement is converted into a value of pension "wealth" using standard actuarial techniques. For each country, the present value of future pension payments is calculated, using a uniform discount rate of 2% and country-specific life expectancy. Since the comparisons refer to prospective pension entitlements, the calculations use national life expectancies as projected for the year 2040.

Countries can more easily afford to promise a higher replacement rate at retirement if the pension eligibility age is higher and so the benefit is paid for a shorter period. The average pension eligibility age in OECD countries is 64.4 for men and 63.9 for women. The calculations use a baseline pension age of 65: this is the most common across OECD countries. The results are shown below for the eight different pension ages that occur in OECD countries, ranging from 58 to 67. For illustration, they are also shown for age 70.

The table below shows the effect on pension wealth of a different pension age for men and women relative to the baseline age of 65, using OECD average mortality rates by age and assuming that the pension in payment is indexed to prices. Setting the pension eligibility age at 64 instead of 65, for example, raises the cost of the long-term pension promise by 3.5%; a retirement age of 67, on the other hand, costs 7% less than retirement at 65.

Pension eligibility age		58	60	62	63	64	65	66	67	70
Pension wealth, relative to baseline (%)	Men	+24.5	+17.5	+10.5	+7.0	+3.5	0.0	−3.5	−7.0	−17.4
	Women	+22.2	+16.1	+9.8	+6.6	+3.3	0.0	−3.3	−6.7	−16.9

France, Korea, and Turkey have a pension eligibility age of 60.[1] For men, a pension paid from age 60 costs 17.5% more than the same benefit paid from age 65. Pension eligibility age has a slightly larger effect on the pension wealth of men than of women. This is because men's shorter life expectancy implies that changes in the pension eligibility age have a proportionally larger effect on the duration of retirement.

These calculations assume that benefits after retirement are adjusted in line with prices. If benefits are linked to the growth of economy-wide average earnings and wages grow faster than prices (following the baseline assumptions), pension wealth will be higher, which means that the pension promise will be more costly.

Indexation procedure		Prices	Earnings	80 p: 20 w	67 p: 33 w	50 p: 50 w
Pension wealth, relative to baseline (%)	Men	0	+21.7	+3.9	+6.5	+10.1
	Women	0	+24.5	+4.3	+7.3	+11.3

Using the baseline assumption of 2% real wage growth, full earnings indexation means that pension wealth is over 20% higher than under price indexation. Full linking of pensions in payment to average earnings is now rare.[2] Indexing to a mix of earnings and prices naturally results in a value of pension wealth which falls between prices up-rating and earnings up-rating. The Czech Republic, Finland, Hungary, Poland, the Slovak Republic and Switzerland all have some type of mixed indexation. For example, the Czech Republic indexes pensions by 67% of price inflation (p) and 33% of wage inflation (w). At the baseline assumptions, this costs around 7% more than a link only to prices.

The effect of more generous indexation procedures is larger for women than for men. This is because of women's longer life expectancy, of over 3½ years on average in OECD countries. This means that they have a longer retirement over which to benefit from the real increases in pension.

The final element in the calculation of pension wealth is the country-specific mortality which, like the pension eligibility age, affects the expected length of retirement. Table 6.1

Table 6.1. **Total life expectancy at age 65, 2040 projected mortality rates**

	Men	Women
Australia	84.0	87.4
Austria	83.7	87.3
Belgium	83.8	87.3
Canada	83.8	87.4
Czech Republic	82.5	86.0
Denmark	83.1	86.0
Finland	83.6	87.5
France	83.9	87.6
Germany	83.2	86.6
Greece	83.3	86.6
Hungary	80.8	85.0
Iceland	84.8	87.5
Ireland	82.8	86.2
Italy	83.0	87.0
Japan	85.8	88.7
Korea	81.8	85.6
Luxembourg	83.0	87.2
Mexico	80.9	84.8
Netherlands	83.5	86.7
New Zealand	83.6	86.8
Norway	84.2	87.5
Poland	81.5	85.6
Portugal	82.8	86.2
Slovak Republic	81.1	85.1
Spain	83.4	87.0
Sweden	84.3	87.5
Switzerland	84.5	88.2
Turkey	80.0	83.0
United Kingdom	83.3	86.4
United States	83.8	87.3
OECD average	**83.1**	**86.6**

Note: These projections build on recent national census data. The assumptions for future changes in mortality rates vary between countries but nonetheless use a consistent methodology. The resulting mortality rates can differ from national projections because of differences in assumptions.

Source: OECD calculations based on United Nations/World Bank population database.

shows the country-specific total life expectancy, separately for men and women, conditional on surviving until age 65. Given that pension entitlements are projected into the future, the calculations use the projections for 2040 from the United Nations/World Bank population database.

Citizens of poorer OECD member states are projected to retain lower life expectancies than their counterparts in richer economies. In Hungary, Mexico, Poland, the Slovak Republic and Turkey, total life expectancy at age 65 is 1½ to three years shorter than the OECD average. Iceland, Japan and Switzerland have significantly longer life expectancy than the OECD mean. The other countries are clustered around the OECD average.

The impact of differences in life expectancy on pension wealth are also quite large. The baseline in the table below is a price-indexed pension paid from age 65 at the OECD average mortality rate. For comparison, the table shows pension wealth calculated using the mortality rates for the five countries with the shortest and the five with the longest life expectancy. Other things being equal, the countries with low life expectancy – Hungary, Mexico, Poland, the Slovak Republic and Turkey – could afford to pay men a pension 10% higher than a country with OECD average mortality rates (Germany, Italy and the United Kingdom, for example). In contrast, longer life expectancies increase the burden on the pension system. For men, pension wealth is nearly 8% higher with the mortality of the five countries with the longest life expectancy, which are Iceland, Japan, Norway, Sweden and Switzerland.

Mortality rates		Best	Average	Worst
Pension wealth, relative to baseline (%)	Men	+7.8	0	−10.2
	Women	+5.0	0	7.4

The results of the calculations of pension wealth at the standard pension age in the respective country are shown in Table 6.2. The pension-wealth numbers show the size of the lump sum that would be needed to buy a flow of pension payments equivalent to that promised by the mandatory pension system in each country. Taking the United States as an example, the mandatory pension for an average earner is worth 5.5 times economy-wide average earnings at the time of retirement. With the exceptions of the countries with purely flat-rate systems – Ireland and New Zealand – pension wealth is smaller for lower earners. At half average earnings in the United States, for example, the mandatory pension is worth 3.5 times economy-wide average earnings.

Luxembourg has the highest pension wealth at every level of earnings. For average and high earners, this is worth double the average for OECD countries.

In countries with shorter life expectancies, such as Hungary, Poland and Turkey, benefits are paid for a shorter retirement period and so the pension promise becomes more affordable. The effect is the reverse in Switzerland and the Nordic countries, where life expectancies are high. Unlike measures of replacement rates, the link between affordability and life expectancy is captured by the pension-wealth indicator.

The effect of pension eligibility ages is also apparent in the results for pension wealth. France, for example, has gross replacement rates below the OECD average at earnings of between 75 and 200% of average. However, pension wealth is above the OECD average at these earnings because the pension eligibility age of 60 is relatively low and life expectancy is a little longer then the OECD mean.

Table 6.2. **Gross pension wealth by earnings level, mandatory pension programmes, men**

Multiple of economy-wide average earnings

	Individual earnings, multiple of average					
	0.5	0.75	1	1.5	2	2.5
Australia	5.7	6.2	6.7	7.7	8.3	8.6
Austria	6.0	9.0	11.9	17.9	19.6	19.6
Belgium	5.5	5.5	7.3	7.5	9.4	9.4
Canada	5.5	6.0	6.5	6.5	6.5	6.5
Czech Republic	4.6	5.2	5.8	6.2	6.6	7.1
Denmark	7.0	7.2	7.4	7.7	8.0	8.3
Finland	6.3	8.4	11.2	16.9	22.5	28.1
France	7.6	7.6	9.5	13.7	17.1	20.5
Germany	4.3	6.2	8.3	12.5	13.7	13.7
Greece	6.3	9.4	12.6	18.9	25.2	31.5
Hungary	6.1	9.1	12.2	18.3	24.4	26.8
Iceland	7.1	7.8	8.4	9.9	12.6	15.3
Ireland	5.4	5.4	5.4	5.4	5.4	5.4
Italy	5.8	8.7	11.4	16.5	22.0	27.5
Japan	5.7	7.0	8.3	10.9	12.2	12.2
Korea	5.0	5.9	6.7	8.4	9.7	9.7
Luxembourg	10.3	14.3	18.3	26.2	34.1	40.2
Mexico	2.6	3.7	4.8	7.0	9.1	11.3
Netherlands	5.2	7.7	10.3	15.5	20.6	25.8
New Zealand	5.7	5.7	5.7	5.7	5.7	5.7
Norway	5.3	6.7	8.2	10.7	11.7	12.1
Poland	4.0	5.9	7.9	11.9	15.8	19.4
Portugal	7.9	7.9	10.2	15.1	20.0	24.7
Slovak Republic	4.0	6.0	8.0	12.0	15.9	19.9
Spain	6.1	9.1	12.2	18.3	23.0	23.0
Sweden	7.0	8.7	10.4	15.5	21.0	26.6
Switzerland	5.5	7.9	10.1	11.5	11.5	11.5
Turkey	6.1	8.5	11.0	15.9	18.2	18.2
United Kingdom	5.0	5.2	5.5	6.6	6.7	6.7
United States	3.5	4.5	5.5	7.1	8.0	8.9
OECD average	**5.7**	**7.2**	**8.9**	**12.1**	**14.8**	**16.8**
With voluntary schemes						
Canada	6.5	8.2	10.2	13.5	16.8	20.1
Denmark	9.3	10.2	11.2	13.1	15.6	18.6
United Kingdom	5.3	6.5	7.7	10.2	12.6	15.0
United States	5.9	8.0	10.0	14.2	17.3	20.4

Source: OECD pension models.

Notes

1. Note that the pension age for women – 58 – is lower than for men in Turkey.

2. However, the value of many first-tier pensions, such as basic and resource-tested schemes, is linked to average earnings.

ISBN 92-64-01871-9
Pensions at a Glance
Public Policies across OECD Countries
© OECD 2005

PART I

Chapter 7

Key Indicators

Building on the results for replacement rates and pension levels across the range of individual earnings, it is possible to develop indicators to address further policy questions in pensions. How much will today's pension promises cost in the future? How much of that cost will be met by the public and private sectors? Answers to these questions require composite indicators of pension systems that aggregate the results for workers at different earnings levels that were presented in Chapters 4 to 6.

1. Weighted averages and the earnings distribution

The technique used to aggregate individual-level results is that of weighted averages. The indicators build on the calculations of pension entitlements for people earning between 0.3 and 3 times the economy-wide average. Each level of individual earnings is given a weight based on its importance in the distribution of earnings. Since there are many people with low earnings, and much fewer with high earnings, low earnings are given a larger weight in the calculation of the indicator than high earnings.

The calculations use the average distribution of earnings based on data[1] for 16 OECD countries, which is shown in Figure 7.1. The chart shows the proportion of employees in these countries whose earnings are a particular proportion of the country-specific average. The earnings distribution is skewed. The mode (or peak) of the distribution is at around two-thirds of mean earnings (referred to as "average" elsewhere in this report). The median (the earnings level both below and above which half of employees are situated) is between 80 and 85% of mean earnings. Two-thirds of people earn less than mean earnings.

Figure 7.1. **Distribution of earnings, average of 16 OECD countries**

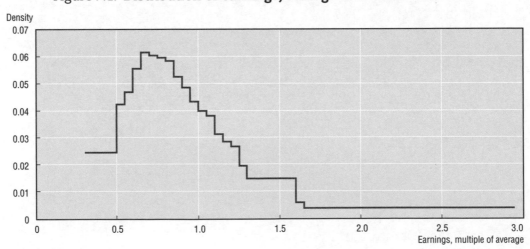

Source: OECD earnings-distribution data.

2. Weighted average pension levels and pension wealth

The measure of *weighted average relative pension level* combines the earnings distribution (Figure 7.1) with the projections of pension entitlements (Chapter 5). The relative pension level is averaged over individuals earning across the range from 0.3 to three times average economy-wide earnings using the earnings-distribution weights. The result is the weighted average of the pension entitlement expressed as a percentage of economy-wide average earnings. This provides a useful indicator of the scale of the pension promise made to today's workers.

This indicator is presented in the first column of Table 7.1. Again, there are vast differences between countries. Nine countries' mandatory systems aim to deliver an average pension of less than 40% of average earnings. These are Australia, Belgium, Canada, Ireland, Korea, Mexico, New Zealand, the United Kingdom and the United States.

Table 7.1. **Weighted average pension level and pension wealth**

Pension level as percentage of economy-wide average earnings, pension wealth as multiple of economy-wide average earnings and in US dollars

	Pension level	Pension wealth		Pension wealth (USD)
		Men	Women	
Australia	39.1	6.6	7.7	189 000
Austria	72.5	11.0	13.3	273 000
Belgium	36.3	6.5	7.5	214 000
Canada	39.9	6.1	7.1	163 000
Czech Republic	41.7	6.9	8.1	47 000
Denmark	43.2	7.3	8.4	304 000
Finland	71.2	11.2	13.3	320 000
France	52.7	9.5	10.9	221 000
Germany	42.6	7.7	9.2	262 000
Greece	83.1	12.4	14.4	144 000
Hungary	72.2	11.7	14.4	55 000
Iceland	53.8	8.6	9.7	256 000
Ireland	30.6	5.4	6.5	143 000
Italy	77.2	11.1	13.1	244 000
Japan	47.9	7.9	8.9	285 000
Korea	39.3	6.5	7.6	129 000
Luxembourg	99.2	17.8	21.9	587 000
Mexico	35.7	4.7	4.5	28 000
Netherlands	67.7	10.2	11.7	316 000
New Zealand	37.6	5.7	6.5	113 000
Norway	49.5	7.7	9.0	306 000
Poland	55.5	7.7	8.1	51 000
Portugal	70.4	10.8	12.6	93 000
Slovak Republic	47.9	7.9	9.6	27 000
Spain	75.4	11.3	13.2	192 000
Sweden	68.5	10.9	12.0	280 000
Switzerland	49.9	8.7	10.7	400 000
Turkey	81.3	10.3	12.2	74 000
United Kingdom	37.1	5.5	6.3	172 000
United States	36.5	5.2	6.1	183 000
OECD average	**55.4**	**8.7**	**10.2**	**202 367**

Note: Weighted averages for the relative pension value and pension wealth use the OECD average earnings distribution. Weighted average pension level is shown for men. Pension wealth in value terms is the simple average of the results for men and women. The conversion to US dollars is performed using 2002 average market exchange rates.

Source: OECD pension models.

At the other extreme, Luxembourg is again an outlier. The weighted average pension there is just slightly less than average earnings. A further three countries have an average relative pension level above 75%: Italy, Spain and Turkey. Next, with pension levels in the low seventies, are Finland, Austria and Hungary.

The same type of weighting can also be applied to the pension wealth measure. The second and third columns of Table 7.1 show the weighted average of pension wealth, separately for men and women. This is the most comprehensive measure of the scale of the pension promise made to today's workers. This is because it takes account of differences in life expectancy, pension eligibility ages and indexation of pensions in payment. The final column of the table also gives these figures in US dollars.

Luxembourg, not surprisingly, has the highest pension wealth, which averages almost 18 times average earnings for men and 22 times for women. This is worth an average of USD 587 000, nearly treble the average for OECD countries. Austria, Finland, Greece, Hungary, Italy and Spain are closely clustered with pension wealth of 11-12 times average earnings. In today's money, average pension wealth is over USD 300 000 in Denmark, Finland, Netherlands, Norway and Switzerland. These numbers represent the present value of the transfers that societies are promising on average to future retirees under the current pension system rules and any reforms that are being phased in over time.

On this comprehensive measure, the most modest pension systems are those of Ireland, Mexico, New Zealand, the United Kingdom and the United States where pension wealth is less than six times average earnings. This is around two-thirds of the average for OECD countries.

The systems of countries with short life expectancies – such as Poland and Turkey – have more modest values for pension wealth compared with other countries. Pension wealth is increased in countries such as France and Hungary because of earlier retirement than is the norm for OECD countries. In France, for example, the weighted average pension level is a little lower than the OECD average while pension wealth is nearly 15% above the average.

3. Structure of the potential resource transfer to pensioners

Table 7.2 shows the contribution that each system component makes to the potential resource transfer to pensioners. These are calculated as the weighted average pension wealth from each source as a percentage of the total.

Eleven countries have basic pension schemes, but their importance in terms of the resource transfer to older people varies substantially. In Ireland and New Zealand, there is only a basic pension; thus, the share is 100%. In Korea, the Netherlands and the United Kingdom, the basic pension makes up around one half of the total resource transfer to pensioners. The earnings-related schemes in Korea and the United Kingdom and occupational plans in the Netherlands make up the other half. Basic pensions in Denmark, Japan and Norway make up around 40% of the transfer.

The resource-tested programmes – social assistance, separate, targeted pension schemes and minimum pensions – also vary hugely in importance. Australia and Denmark rely mostly on these types of schemes, with over 40% of the transfer going on these benefits. In Iceland, the total for the two resource-tested pensions is nearly 40%.[2] Targeted schemes play a modest though significant role in the Sweden and Turkey with a similar degree of reliance on the minimum credits in the Belgian scheme.

Table 7.2. **Contribution of different components of pension systems to total pension promise**

Percentage of total weighted average pension wealth

Tier: function	First tier: universal coverage, redistributive				Second tier: mandatory, insurance		
Provision	Public					Private	
Type	Social assistance	Targeted	Basic	Minimum	Public	DB	DC
Australia		45.0					55.0
Austria		1.0			99.0		
Belgium				11.1[1]	88.9		
Canada		15.8	34.3		49.8		
Czech Republic			18.3		81.7		
Denmark		41.4	41.1		9.2		8.3
Finland		1.6			98.4		
France		6.5			93.6[2]		
Germany	1.9				98.1		
Greece							
Hungary					66.4		33.6
Iceland		37.8[3]				62.2	
Ireland			100.0				
Italy					100.0		
Japan			39.5		60.5		
Korea			51.6[4]		48.4		
Luxembourg			13.6[5]	0.2	86.2		
Mexico	1.1						98.9[6]
Netherlands			50.7			49.3	
New Zealand			100.0				
Norway		1.3	41.4		57.4		
Poland		0.6			47.3		52.1
Portugal				4.2	95.8		
Slovak Republic				0.7	99.3		
Spain				0.5	99.5		
Sweden		8.6			49.1	23.3	18.9[7]
Switzerland		0.4			66.6	33.1	
Turkey		10.2			89.8		
United Kingdom			54.4	35.1[8]	10.5		
United States					100.0		

DB: Defined benefit.

DC: Defined contribution.

1. Belgium: the minimum pension also includes minimum credits.
2. France: public, second-tier pension is made up of the state pension (63.5%) plus the ARRCO occupational scheme (30.1%).
3. Iceland: there are two targeted schemes: the basic pension and the supplement (18.1% and 19.7% respectively).
4. Korea: the basic column shows the benefit related to average rather than individual earnings.
5. Luxembourg: the basic figure also includes the small end-of-year allowance.
6. Mexico: DC flat-rate contribution provides 8.9% and the variable contribution 90.0%.
7. Sweden: the two DC schemes are the state-mandated contribution (10.6%) and the DC part of the occupational pension (8.3%).
8. United Kingdom: minimum pension refers to minimum credits in state second pension.

Source: OECD pension models.

Elsewhere, first-tier schemes play little or no role in providing pensions for full-career workers (although they tend to be important for workers with partial careers). All or practically all of the resource transfer is in public, earnings-related provision in Austria, Finland, Germany, Italy, the Slovak Republic, Spain and the United States.

Notes

1. The data are decile points of the earnings distribution and mean earnings. They are gross earnings of full-time workers, including men and women. This definition was chosen to approximate as closely as possible the earnings of the average production worker used in models of both pension entitlements and worker and pensioner taxation.

2. There is a third means-tested scheme in Iceland but this is not relevant for a full-career worker.

the accumulated notional capital is increased each year by the notional interest rate. At
age is equal to the pension-point value to the ratio of the notional
accounts contribution to the annuity factor, respectively.

ANNEX I.1

Differences between Defined-benefit, Points and Notional-accounts Pension Systems

This report has grouped together publicly provided, earnings-related pension schemes of
three broad types. This annex provides a brief analysis of the difference between these
three different programmes using some basic algebra.

A simple, generic **defined-benefit scheme** pays a constant accrual rate, a, for each
year of service. It is based on lifetime average revalued earnings. The pension benefit can
therefore be written as:

$$DB = \sum_{i=o}^{R} w_i (1+u)^{R-i} a$$

where w_i are individual earnings in a particular year, R is the year of retirement and u is the
factor by which earlier years' earnings are revalued. In most OECD countries, this is the
growth of economy-wide average earnings.

In a **points system**, pension points are calculated by dividing earnings by the cost of
the pension point (k). The pension benefit then depends on the value of a point at the time
of retirement, v. Thus, the pension benefit can be written as:

$$PP = \sum_{i=o}^{R} \frac{w_i v_R}{k_i}$$

A significant public-policy variable is the policy for uprating the value of the pension
point, shown by the parameter x. By writing the pension-point value at the time of
retirement as a function of its contemporaneous value, $v_R = v_i (1+x)^{R-i}$, the equation becomes:

$$PP = \sum_{i=o}^{R} \frac{w_i v_i}{k_i} (1+x)^{R-i} a$$

The inflow to **notional accounts** each year is wages multiplied by the contribution
rate. The notional capital is increased each year by the notional interest rate, n. At
retirement, the accumulated notional capital is divided by a notional annuity factor, A,
sometimes called the g-value. The pension benefit can be written as:

$$NA = \sum_{i=o}^{R} \frac{w_i c}{A} (1+n)^{R-i}$$

All the schemes are clearly earnings-related, since their value depends deterministically
on individual earnings, w. Furthermore, if the policy for valorising earlier years' earnings is
the same as the uprating procedure for the pension point and the notional interest rate, then

the structure of the three equations is very similar. In this case, the defined-benefit accrual rate is equal to the ratio of the pension-point value to its cost and to the ratio of the notional-accounts contribution rate to the annuity factor, or algebraically:

$$a = \frac{v_i}{k_i} = \frac{c}{A}$$

This has two implications for the comparison of these different types of pension scheme. First, the effective accrual rate can be calculated for pension-point schemes (the ratio of point value to cost) and notional-accounts schemes (the ratio of the contribution rate to the annuity factor). The results of this calculation are shown in Table 2.1 in Chapter 2. Secondly, the valorisation procedure in defined-benefit schemes, the uprating policy for the pension-point value and setting the notional interest rate are exactly parallel policies (as they are presented in Table 2.2 in Chapter 2). Different choices of variables have the same effect in the different types of systems.

Although defined-benefit, points and notional-accounts systems can appear very different, they are in fact closely related variants of earnings-related pension schemes.

ANNEX I.2

Sensitivity Analyses

1. Varying rates of return on defined-contribution pensions

Six OECD member countries have defined-contribution (DC) pensions. Pension entitlements in DC schemes depend crucially on the rate of return earned by the contributions when they are invested. The baseline assumption of the modelling is that the real return earned by DC pensions is 3.5% per year. This is a relatively conservative assumption by historical, empirical standards. Between 1984 and 1996, real rates of return of pension funds in eight OECD countries averaged 8% per year (OECD, 1998, Table V.3).

Nonetheless, some commentators argue that the risk-adjusted rate of return on defined-contribution pensions cannot exceed the riskless interest rate (for example, Bodie, 1995). This variable, which underlies the actuarial calculations in this report, is assumed to be 2%. On the other hand, other analysts argue that there is an "equity premium" that delivers higher returns than the riskless interest rate even allowing for the costs of the risk borne. These issues have generated a substantial literature.[1]

Given the uncertainty about future rates of return on DC pensions, pension entitlements have been modelled using a wide range of real returns, from zero to 6%. The total pension entitlement is shown in Figure I.2.1 including all pension sources. The figures show the replacement rate for low, average and high earners (defined as earning half, average and twice average) under different assumptions for the real rate of return.

Overall pension entitlements in countries with substantial DC schemes are most sensitive to earnings in Mexico. This is because other countries have more substantial public pensions (which, of course, do not vary with the rate of return) than the Mexican minimum pension. A high rate of return (6%) would virtually double the value of Mexican pension entitlements relative to the baseline assumption (of 3.5%). The effect of a lower return than in the baseline is similar: a rate of return of zero cuts benefits by one half compared with the baseline for average and high earners. Low earners, however, are protected from the effects of a lower rate of return by the minimum pension. A similar effect can be observed for low earners in Poland.

Pension entitlements in other countries are less sensitive to the rate of return. In Hungary, for example, the pension is only 25% higher with the maximum rate of return. This is because two-thirds of the pension package under the baseline assumptions comes from the public pension (Table 7.2). In Australia, the effect of the rate of return is muted by the means test in the public pension system. Even high earners are entitled to some age pension. This means that, for each extra dollar of income from the defined-contribution

Figure I.2.1. **Total gross replacement rates for low, average and high earners by rate of return on defined-contribution pensions**

As a proportion of individual earnings

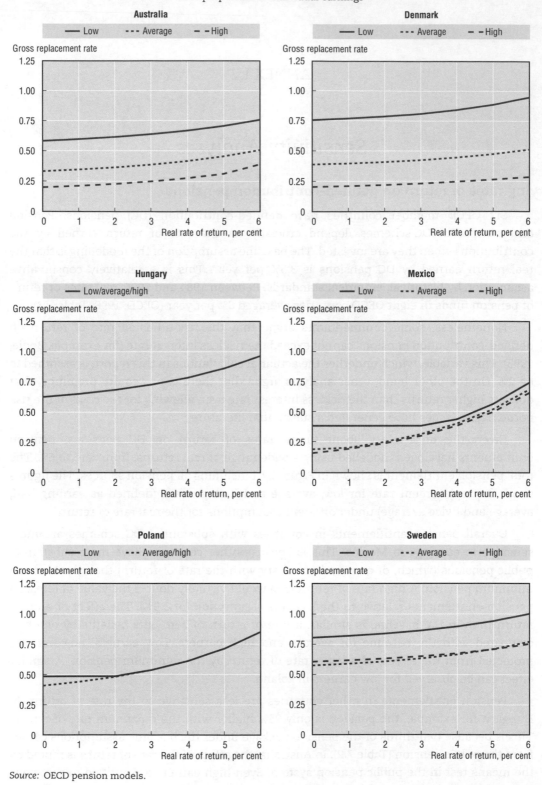

Source: OECD pension models.

plan, 40 cents of age pension is withdrawn. Similarly, in Sweden, the income-tested guarantee pension covers both the low and average-income earner on the baseline assumptions. This, coupled with the relatively small contribution to the two defined-contribution schemes, means that the overall pension benefit is least sensitive to the rate of return in Sweden of all the six countries with mandatory defined-contribution plans.

Most of the countries with mandatory DC plans have various types of guarantees of either the pension value or the rate of return that individual accounts earn. These guarantees are additional to the protection afforded by various public pension programmes, including minimum pensions.[2] They are financed in many different ways, including resources within the pension fund, the capital of the pension-fund manager, a central guarantee fund and the government's general budget.

Hungary and Mexico offer absolute guarantees of the pension level. Conditional on a contribution history of 15 years, the government in Hungary guarantees that the annuity bought from the DC accumulation will be at least 25% of the benefit under the public, earnings-related pension scheme. Mexico transferred all workers to the new private scheme. The guarantee is that the government will make up the difference if the annuity provided by the private scheme is lower than the benefit that they would have received under the old regime. Indeed, most people nearing retirement at present are virtually certain to trigger the guarantee.

Poland provides a different kind of guarantee: on the rate of return earned by a particular pension fund relative to the rates of return earned by other pension funds. The guarantee is that returns are at least the smaller of 50% of all funds' average nominal return and the average nominal return minus 4%. Hungary also has a relative rate-of-return guarantee: that the return must be better than 15 percentage points below the return on an index of government bonds.

The effect of these guarantees on individual pension entitlements is impossible to model with any reasonable precision, because it depends both on the performance of capital-markets as a whole and the outcomes delivered by particular pension funds.[3]

2. Varying real rates of growth of economy-wide average earnings

In the great majority of the earnings-related pension systems in OECD member countries, earlier years' earnings are adjusted (or "valorised") in line with economy-wide average earnings when calculating benefits (Table 2.2 in Chapter 2). In these cases, the results (for replacement rates, pension wealth, etc.) are insensitive to variations in the assumption for economy-wide wage growth. If wages grow faster than the baseline assumption, then earlier years' earnings will be revalued by a larger amount, leaving the replacement rate and other indicators unchanged.

However, a small number of countries valorise earnings in a less generous way than adjusting individual earlier years' earnings in line with economy-wide earnings growth. In Belgium, the French public scheme, Korea and Spain, earlier years' earnings are valorised in line with prices. In Portugal, valorisation is mixed: 75% to prices and 25% to earnings with a maximum uplift of 0.5% per year.

There are policies in points and notional-accounts schemes that are the parallel of valorisation in DB plans. In the French occupational plan, the uprating policy for the value of the pension point (which has the same effect as valorisation in defined-benefit schemes) is also linked to prices. In Poland, the notional interest rate (again the parallel of valorisation) is currently prices plus 75% of growth in the real wage bill. In all these cases, the value of pension entitlements is sensitive to the assumption for economy-wide average earnings growth. Faster growth of earnings means that pension entitlements of earlier years fall further behind individual wages, meaning that replacement rate and relative pension level are lower.

Figure I.2.2 shows pension replacement rates at different assumptions for average earnings growth, ranging from zero to 3% per year. (The baseline assumption is for 2% annual earnings growth.) Replacement rates are shown for low, average and high earners (that is, half, average and double average pay).

In Belgium and Portugal, low-income workers are protected from the effects of variations in earnings growth by minimum pension credits and minimum pensions respectively. Overall, pensions are most sensitive to this assumption in Belgium. This is because the public pension is based on lifetime average earnings, which maximises the impact. In the French public scheme, in contrast, the earnings measure is the best 25 years and in Spain, it is the final 15 years. This mutes the impact compared with Belgium. In Poland and Portugal, the sensitivity is lessened by the partial valorisation to earnings. At average earnings, the effect of earnings growth of three rather than 2% is to cut the replacement rate by 15% in Belgium, 13% in Poland and Portugal, 12% in France and 6% in Spain.

3. Varying individual career earnings paths

The great majority of OECD countries use lifetime average earnings to calculate earnings-related pension benefits. This, coupled with a policy of earnings valorisation of earlier years' pay, means that pension entitlements are insensitive to the shape of the individual career earnings path. An individual with a steeper age-earnings profile will receive the same benefit relative to lifetime average revalued earnings. In some countries, however, pension benefits are calculated based on a limited number of best or final years' pay. In the French public scheme, benefits are currently based on the best 20 years' earnings, which will gradually move to 25 years. Similarly, Norwegian pensions are based on the best 20 years' points. In Spain, the earnings measure is the final 15 years. Finally, results are also shown for Belgium, which uses lifetime average pay, to show the effect of a policy of prices valorisation in isolation.

Figure I.2.3 shows how pension entitlements vary with individual earnings growth relative to the economy-wide average. The baseline results assume that individual earnings growth over the career tracks the economy-wide average, implying that the baseline assumption is zero in these figures.[4] As in the previous sensitivity analyses, low and high earnings are defined as half and double the average.

The impact of career earnings profiles is most marked in Spain because Spain has the shortest period over which pensionable earnings are measured. Individual earnings growth of 1% ahead of average earnings across the career gives a pension 16% larger than the baseline assumption that individual earnings grow in line with the average.

The effect is also quite large for the average earner in Norway, where the averaging period is 20 years. However, it is muted for high earners by the effect of the pension ceiling and for low earners by the basic and resource-tested benefits.

Figure I.2.2. **Total gross replacement rates for low, average and high earners by rate of growth of economy-wide average earnings**

As a proportion of individual earnings

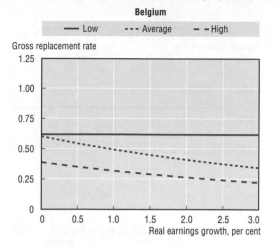

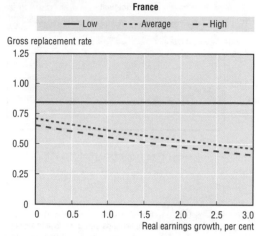

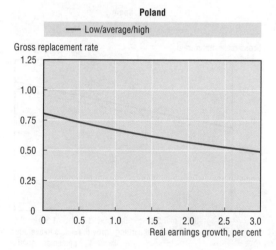

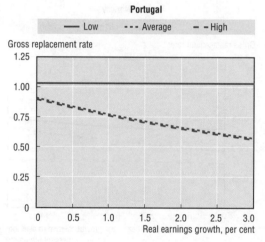

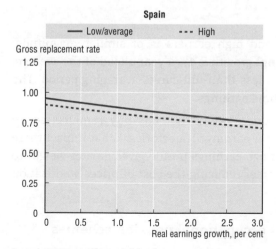

Source: OECD pension models.

Figure I.2.3. **Total gross replacement rates for low, average and high earners by rate of growth of individual earnings relative to average earnings**

As a proportion of individual earnings

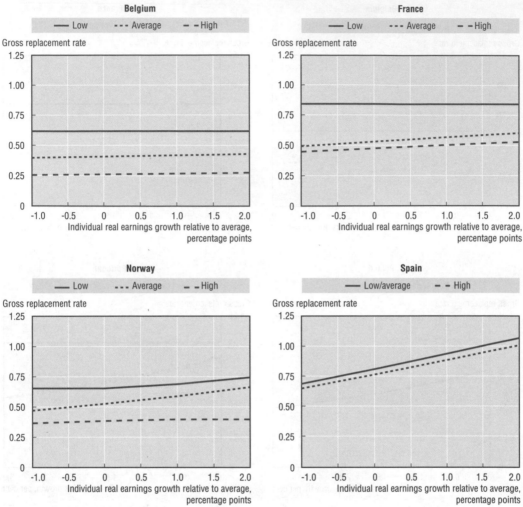

Source: OECD pension models.

In France, the impact on the average and high earners is of similar magnitude: around 6% higher benefits if individual earnings growth is 1% a year ahead of the average. This is because only the public scheme uses a less-than-full-career averaging period. The occupational plan, based on points, uses lifetime earnings.

Finally, the results for Belgium show that prices valorisation has only a small effect on the sensitivity of the results to individual career earnings trajectories. What impact there is can be explained by the fact that a steeper age-earnings profile gives greater weight to individual earnings towards the end of the career reducing the cost of prices valorisation on benefits.

4. Varying number of jobs in defined-benefit occupational pension schemes

Some results in the main body of this report include defined-benefit (DB) occupational schemes; these are discussed in detail after the country studies. DB occupational plans tend to use final salary as the earnings measure for calculating benefits. The earnings measure has a much greater effect on benefits in occupational schemes than in national pension plans because the relevant "final" salary is that with a particular employer and so not usually the same as earnings just before retirement. The value of benefits is therefore eroded substantially for people who leave their employer before retirement. It is unrealistic to assume that people remain with the same employer all of their working life when this is not and never has been common. Moreover, this assumption exaggerates the value of pension benefits from occupational plans enormously.

In the United Kingdom, pensions of "early leavers" must be uprated in line with price inflation, but this still can reduce benefits (compared with the growth of accrued pension rights for people staying until retirement in line with their own earnings).[5] In Canada and the United States, there is not even this limited degree of protection of the pension rights of early leavers.

The baseline results assume that individuals join four different pension schemes even though they are covered by occupational pensions for all of their career.

There are two main problems with using these data as an indication of the length of time people spend in a particular occupational pension plan. First, they relate to incomplete tenures in the current job, not final tenures (when people change jobs). This problem, known as "right-censoring" in econometric analysis of duration data, means that it is impossible to know the distribution of completed tenures in advance. Secondly, the job-tenure pattern of members of final-salary occupational pensions differs from that of the population as a whole; the survey data cited above cannot distinguish whether people are members of occupational plans or not. Indeed, many analysts have viewed final-salary pensions as a device for employers to reducing costly mobility of their employees.[6]

The analysis that follows therefore considers a range of different job tenures. In each case, the working life is divided equally between a number of different jobs, ranging from one to 10. A full career with a single employer for an average earner would give an overall replacement rate (including public pensions) of 109% in the United States, 96% in Canada and 76% in the United Kingdom (Figure I.2.4).

Already with two jobs over the career, the overall pension would be 16% lower in the United Kingdom and around 20% lower in both Canada and the United States. This difference is because of the preservation rules in the United Kingdom, which require price indexation of benefits between leaving a job and drawing the pension.

Greater job mobility (that two career jobs) reduces pension benefits still further. However, once the number of jobs is five or more, the loss of pension rights with greater mobility becomes negligible. Pension benefits relative to a full career with a single employer are around 25% lower in the United Kingdom and 30% lower in Canada and the United States. In Canada, the public schemes (basic, resource-tested and earnings-related) mean that low-income workers do not see much effect from increased job mobility on overall pension entitlement. This is also the case because of the progressive structure of the public, earnings-related schemes in the United Kingdom and the United States and the basic pension in the former. However, the relationship is not as strong as it is in Canada.

Figure I.2.4. **Total gross replacement rates for low, average and high earners by the number of jobs over the career**

As a proportion of individual earnings

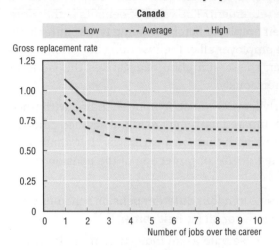

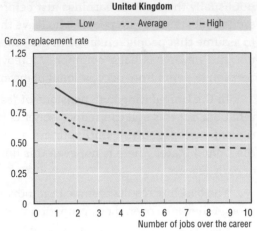

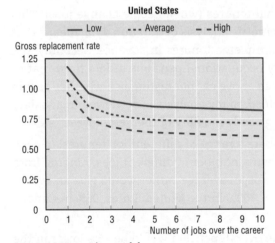

Source: OECD pension models.

Notes

1. See, *inter alia*, Blanchard (1993), Constantinides, Donaldson and Mehra (1998), Jagannathan and Kocherlakota (1996) and Mehra and Prescott (1985).

2. See Palacios and Whitehouse (2000) on the types of guarantee provided by different countries and their financing.

3. There are also important implications for the public finances from these explicit (as well as implicit) guarantees of pension outcomes in a defined-contribution world. See Pennachi (1998) for a discussion.

4. See the section "What Do True Age-earnings Profiles Look Like?" in Disney and Whitehouse (1999) for a discussion of different assumptions.

5. Employers in the United Kingdom were prohibited from simply returning employees' pension contributions if they left before normal retirement age from 1975. Benefits had to be "preserved" in the scheme, but their value was related to salary at the time of leaving and not adjusted for inflation. Preserved pensions accrued after 1985 were required to be up-rated in line with prices, up to a ceiling of 5%; in 1990 this was extended to the whole pension, not just the part accrued after 1985. See Whitehouse (1998) for a discussion.

6. Examples include Lazear (1981, 1985), Viscusi (1985) and Ippolito (1991). See Palacios and Whitehouse (2004), Section 2 in Chapter 3 for a detailed survey.

ANNEX I.3

Progressivity of Pension Benefit Formulae

The charts in Figure 5.1 of Chapter 5 show how the pattern of pension entitlements varies with earnings for different countries. This illustrates the very different philosophies of different pension systems, particularly in their relative emphasis on the insurance and redistributive roles of pension systems. The allocation of countries to six groups (Figures 5.1A to 5.1F) depends on the strength of the link between pre-retirement earnings and post-retirement pension entitlements. It is based on a single summary indicator, the calculation methodology and results of which are presented here.

Consider two benchmark regimes. The first is termed a "pure basic" scheme. It pays the same flat-rate amount to all pensioners regardless both of their earnings history and their other sources of income. Such a scheme is sometimes also called a "demogrant" or a "citizen's pension". The relative pension value is independent of earnings (as illustrated in Figure 5.1A for the flat-rate systems of Ireland and New Zealand) and the replacement rate declines with earnings.

At the other end of the spectrum of benefit design is a "pure insurance" scheme. This aims to pay the same replacement rate to all workers when they retire. The pension value obviously increases with earnings in a straight line, which is why these plans are often called "linear". Defined-contribution plans typically conform to this pure-insurance model because the contribution rate is usually a constant proportion of earnings for all workers (the only exception is Mexico). Many earnings-related schemes (of the defined-benefit, points and notional-accounts varieties) are also linear: they offer the same accrual rate to most workers regardless of earnings, years of service or age.

These two benchmarks – pure-insurance and pure-basic schemes – underpin an "index of progressivity" constructed for cross-country comparison of pension benefit formulae. The index is designed so that a pure basic scheme would score 100% and a pure insurance scheme, zero. The former is maximally progressive; the latter is not progressive since the replacement rate is constant.

The calculation is based on the Gini coefficient, which is a measure of inequality and is widely used in studies of income distribution. The higher the Gini coefficient, the more unequal a distribution. Formally, the index of progressivity is calculated as 100 minus the ratio of the Gini coefficient of pension entitlements divided by the Gini coefficient of earnings (expressed as percentages). In each case, the Gini coefficients are calculated using the earnings distribution as the weight. Table I.3.1 shows the calculation both with national data (where available) and with the OECD average for the earnings distribution (see Figure 7.1 in Chapter 7).

Table I.3.1. **Indicators of the progressivity of pension benefit formulae**

Gini coefficient for pension entitlements and progressivity index for OECD average
and national earnings distributions

| | Earnings distribution | | | |
| | OECD average | | National | |
	Gini	Index	Gini	Index
Australia	6.8	74.8	6.8	78.9
Austria	21.5	20.7		
Belgium	9.5	64.8		
Canada	3.7	86.5		
Czech Republic	7.8	71.1	7.5	76.8
Denmark	2.3	91.7		
Finland	25.3	6.7	22.6	29.9
France	14.6	46.4		
Germany	20.9	22.9	19.8	38.8
Greece	26.0	4.3		
Hungary	25.6	5.6		
Iceland	10.6	60.8		
Ireland	0.0	100.0	0.0	100
Italy	26.1	4.0	22.5	30.4
Japan	14.2	47.8	13.9	56.8
Korea	11.7	56.9	12.9	60
Luxembourg	22.5	17.2		
Mexico	23.4	13.7		
Netherlands	25.6	5.7	24.4	24.4
New Zealand	0.0	100.0	0.0	100
Norway	14.8	45.3	11.8	63.5
Poland	25.7	5.2	27.2	15.6
Portugal	18.7	31.1		
Slovak Republic	26.3	3.2		
Spain	23.6	13.0	26.7	17.3
Sweden	21.3	21.6	18.1	44
Switzerland	15.2	44.1		
Turkey	20.5	24.4		
United Kingdom	8.3	69.6	9.3	67.1
United States	16.1	40.6	19.4	40
OECD average	**16.4**	**39.5**	**15.2**	**52.7**

Source: OECD pension models.

The first column of Table I.3.1 shows the results for the Gini coefficient of gross pension benefits. The second column shows the index of progressivity of the benefit formula. In the flat-rate cases – Ireland and New Zealand – the index is, as explained above, 100. Other countries with highly progressive pension systems are Australia, Canada, the Czech Republic, Denmark and the United Kingdom where the index is above two thirds. These countries all have targeted or basic pensions that play a major role in retirement-income provision.

At the other end of the scale, Finland, Hungary, Italy, the Netherlands, Poland and the Slovak Republic have almost entirely proportional systems with very limited progressivity. The index is less than 10 in all these cases. This group includes two of the countries with notional accounts, which were deliberately designed to have a close link between contributions and benefits. Other countries lie between these two groups.

Note that these calculations are only based on the outcomes of the mandatory parts of the pension systems. In practice, countries that have a voluntary element for higher earners – for example the United Kingdom – will also have more extensive private occupational and personal pension provision. Taking these into account makes the overall distribution of pensioners' incomes wider than that based only on the mandatory pensions.

Bibliography

Aldrich, J. (1982), "The Earnings Replacement Rate of Old-age Benefits in Twelve Countries: 1969-1980", *Social Security Bulletin*, Vol. 45, No. 11, pp. 3-11.

Blanchard, O.J. (1993), "The Vanishing Equity Premium", in R. O'Brien (ed.), *Finance and the International Economy 7*, Oxford University Press.

Bodie, Z. (1995), "On the Risk of Stocks in the Long Run", *Financial Analysts' Journal*, May-June, pp. 18-22.

Casey, B., H. Oxley, E.R. Whitehouse, P. Antolín, R. Duval and W. Leibfritz (2003), "Policies for an Ageing Society: Recent Measures and Areas for Further Reform", Economics Department Working Paper No. 369, OECD, Paris.

Cichon, M. (1999), "Notional Defined-contribution Schemes: Old Wine in new Bottles?", *International Social Security Review*, Vol. 52, No. 4, pp. 87-105.

Constantinides, G., J. Donaldson and R. Mehra (1998), "'Junior Can't Borrow' A New Perspective on the Equity Premium Puzzle", Working Paper No. 6617, National Bureau of Economic Research, Cambridge.

Dang, T.T., P. Antolín and H. Oxley (2001), "Fiscal Implications of Ageing: Projections of Age-related Spending", Working Paper No. 305, Economics Department, OECD, Paris.

Diamond, P.A. (1997), "Insulation of Pensions from Political Risk", in S. Valdés-Prieto (ed.), *The Economics of Pensions: Principles, Policies and International Experience*, Cambridge University Press.

Disney, R.F. (1999), "Notional Accounts as a Pension Reform Strategy: an Evaluation", Pension Reform Primer Series, Social Protection Discussion Paper No. 9928, World Bank, Washington, D.C.

Disney, R.F. and P.G. Johnson (eds.) (2001), *Pension Systems and Retirement Incomes Across OECD Countries*, Edward Elgar, Aldershot.

Disney, R.F. and Whitehouse, E.R. (1994), "Choice of Private Pension and Pension Benefits in Britain", Working Paper No. 94/2, Institute for Fiscal Studies, London.

Disney, R.F. and E.R. Whitehouse (1996), "What are Pension Plan Entitlements Worth in Britain?", *Economica*, Vol. 63, pp. 213-238.

Disney, R.F. and E.R. Whitehouse (1999), "Pension Plans and Retirement Incentives", Pension Reform Primer Series, Social Protection Discussion Paper No. 9924, World Bank, Washington, D.C.

Disney, R.F. and E.R. Whitehouse (2001), *Cross-Country Comparisons of Pensioners' Incomes*, Report Series No. 142, Department for Work and Pensions, London.

Eurostat (1993), *Old Age Replacement Ratios*, Vol. 1, *Relation between Pensions and Income from Employment at the Moment of Retirement*, Statistical Office of the European Communities, Luxembourg.

Finkelstein, A. and J. Poterba (2002), "Selection Effects in the United Kingdom Individual Annuities Market", *Economic Journal*, Vol. 112, No. 476, pp. 28-50.

Finkelstein, A. and J. Poterba (2004), "Adverse Selection in Insurance Markets: Policyholder Evidence from the UK Annuity Market", *Journal of Political Economy*, Vol. 112, No. 1, pp. 183-208.

Förster, M.F. and M. Mira d'Ercole (2005), "Income Distribution and Poverty in OECD Countries in the Second Half of the 1990s", Social, Employment and Migration Working Paper, No. 22, OECD, Paris.

Hernanz, V., F. Malherbert and M. Pellizzari (2004), "Take-up of Welfare Benefits in OECD Countries: a Review of the Evidence", Social, Employment and Migration Working Paper No. 17, OECD, Paris.

Ippolito, R. (1991), "Encouraging Long Tenure: Wage Tilt or Pensions", *Industrial and Labor Relations Review*, Vol. 44, No. 3.

Jagannathan, R. and N. Kocherlakota (1996), "Why Should Older People Invest Less in Stocks than Younger People?", *Federal Reserve Bank of Minneapolis Quarterly Review*, Vol. 20, No. 3, Summer.

Johnson, P.G. (1998), *Older Getting Wiser*, Institute of Chartered Accountants in Australia.

Keenay, G. and E.R. Whitehouse (2002a), "Taxing Pensioners", in *Taxing Wages*, OECD, Paris.

Keenay, G. and E.R. Whitehouse (2002b), "The Role of the Personal Tax System in Old-age Support: a Survey of 15 Countries", Discussion Paper No. 02/07, Centre for Pensions and Superannuation, University of New South Wales, Sydney.

Keenay, G. and E.R. Whitehouse (2003a), "Financial Resources and Retirement in Nine OECD Countries: the Role of the Tax System", Social, Employment and Migration Working Paper No. 8, OECD, Paris.

Keenay, G. and E.R. Whitehouse (2003b), "The Role of the Personal Tax System in Old-age Support: a Survey of 15 Countries", *Fiscal Studies*, Vol. 24, No. 1, pp. 1-21.

Lazear, E. (1981), "Agency, Earnings Profiles, Productivity and Hours Restrictions", *American Economic Review*, Vol. 71, pp. 606-620.

Lazear, E. (1985), "Incentive Effects of Pensions", in D. Wise (ed.), *Pensions, Labor and Individual Choice*, University of Chicago Press for National Bureau of Economic Research.

McHale, J. (1999), "The Risk of Social Security Benefit Rule Changes: Some International Evidence", Working Paper No. 7031, National Bureau of Economic Research, Cambridge, Mass.

Mehra, R. and E.C. Prescott (1985), "The Equity Premium: a puzzle", *Journal of Monetary Economics*, Vol. 15, pp. 145-161.

Mitchell, O.S. and E.L. Dykes (2000), "New Trends in Pension Benefit and Retirement Provisions", Working Paper No. 2000-1, Pension Research Council, Wharton School, University of Pennsylvania, Philadelphia.

OECD (1995), *Private Pensions in OECD Countries: Canada*, Social Policy Studies No. 15, Paris.

OECD (2001), *Ageing and Income. Financial Resources and Retirement in Nine OECD Countries*, Paris.

OECD (2003), *Taxing Wages*, Paris.

OECD (2004), *OECD Classification and Glossary of Private Pensions*, Paris.

OECD (2005), *Taxing Wages*, Paris.

Palacios, R.J. and E.R. Whitehouse (2000), "Guarantees: Counting the Cost of Guaranteeing Defined Contribution Pensions", Pension Reform Primer briefing note, World Bank, Washington, D.C.

Palacios, R.J. and E.R. Whitehouse (2005), "Civil-service Pension Schemes Around the World", Pension Reform Primer series, Social Protection Discussion Paper, World Bank, Washington, D.C., forthcoming.

Pennachi, G.G. (1998), "Government Guarantees on Funded Pension Returns", Pension Reform Primer series, Social Protection Discussion Paper No. 9806, World Bank.

Turner, J.A. and D.M. Rajnes (2000), "Limiting Worker Financial Risk Through Risk Sharing: Minimum Rate of Return Guarantees for Mandatory Defined Contribution Plans", International Labour Organisation, Geneva.

United Kingdom, Department of Work and Pensions (2003), "Income Related Benefits Estimates of Take-up – 2000-2001", London.

United Kingdom, Government Actuary's Department (2003), *Occupational Pension Schemes in 2000: Eleventh Survey by the Government Actuary*.

United States, Department of Labor (1999), *Private Pension Plan Bulletin: Abstract of 1996 Form 5 500 Annual Reports*, Pension and Welfare Benefits Administration, Washington, D.C.

Viscusi, W.K. (1985), "The Structure of Uncertainty and the Use of Pensions as a Mobility-reduction Device", in D. Wise (ed.), *Pensions, Labor and Individual Choice*, University of Chicago Press for National Bureau of Economic Research.

Vordring, H. and Goudswaard, K. (1997), "Indexation of Public Pension Benefits on a Legal Basis: Some Experiences in European Countries", *International Social Security Review*, Vol. 50, No. 3, pp. 31-44.

Weaver, R.K. (1988), *Automatic Government: The Politics of Indexation*, Brookings Institution, Washington, D.C.

Whiteford, P. (1995), "The Use of Replacement Rates in International Comparisons of Benefit Systems", *International Social Security Review*, Vol. 48, No. 2.

Whitehouse, E.R. (1998), "Pension Reform in Britain", Pension Reform primer series, Social Protection Discussion Paper No. 9810, World Bank, Washington, D.C.

Whitehouse, E.R. (2000), "Administrative Charges for Funded Pensions: Measurement Concepts, International Comparison and Assessment", *Journal of Applied Social Science Studies*, Vol. 120, No. 3, pp. 311-361.

Whitehouse, E.R. (2001), "Administrative Charges for Funded Pensions: Comparison and Assessment of 13 Countries", in *Private Pension Systems: Administrative Costs and Reforms, Private Pensions Series*, Vol. 3, OECD, Paris.

Whitehouse, E.R. (2002), "Pension Systems in 15 Countries Compared: the Value of Entitlements", Discussion Paper No. 02/04, Centre for Pensions and Superannuation, University of New South Wales, Sydney.

Whitehouse, E.R. (2005a), "Pension Policy Around the World: Vol. 1, High-income OECD Countries", Social Protection Discussion Paper, World Bank, Washington, D.C.

Whitehouse, E.R. (2005b), "Pension Policy Around the World: Vol. 2, Eastern Europe and Central Asia", Social Protection Discussion Paper, World Bank, Washington, D.C.

Whitehouse, E.R. (2005c), "Pension Policy Around the World: Vol. 3, Latin American and Caribbean", Social Protection Discussion Paper, World Bank, Washington, D.C.

Whitehouse, E.R. and R.J. Palacios (2005), "Pension Policy Around the World: Vol. 5, South Asian Civil-service Schemes", Social Protection Discussion Paper, World Bank, Washington, D.C.

Whitehouse, E.R. and D. Robalino (2005), "Pension Policy Around the World: Vol. 4, Middle East and North Africa", Social Protection Discussion Paper, World Bank, Washington, D.C.

World Bank (1994), *Averting the Old-Age Crisis: Policies to Protect the Old and Promote Growth*, Oxford University Press.

PART II

Country Studies

ISBN 92-64-01871-9
Pensions at a Glance
Public Policies across OECD Countries
© OECD 2005

Introduction

The country studies follow a standard schema. First, there is a detailed description of the rules and parameters of the pension schemes:*

- Qualifying conditions: pension eligibility (or "retirement") age and years of contributions required to receive a pension.

- Benefit calculation: the rules for each schemes making up the pension system, such as earnings-related schemes, mandatory private plans and resource-tested schemes.

- Treatment of pensioners under the personal income tax and social security contributions, including any reliefs for pension income.

- Economic variables: the earnings of the average production worker in local currency and, using the market and the purchasing-power-parity exchange rates shown, converted into US dollars.

Values of the parameters of pension, tax and social security contribution systems are given in national currencies and as a proportion of average earnings. (Note that these are the earnings of the average production worker as set out in the OECD, 2003, *Taxing Wages* report. The values used are shown in Section 4 of Chapter 3.) Parameter values in national currencies are generally rounded to the nearest currency unit.

A summary results table gives relative pension values, replacement rates and pension wealth at different individual levels of earnings. These are given in both gross and net terms (the latter taking account of taxes and contributions paid when working and when drawing the pension). Summary charts show the breakdown of the gross relative pension value into the different components of the pension scheme (the first row of the charts). As far as possible, the same, consistent terminology is used to describe these schemes. (This was set out in Chapter 1 on pension-system typology.) The particular national scheme that is described can be found in the text of the country study. Some standard abbreviations are used in the legends of the charts:

- SA: social assistance.

- Targeted: separate resource-tested schemes for older people.

- Minimum: a minimum pension within an earnings related scheme.

- Basic: a pension based only on number of years of coverage or residency.

- Earnings-related: all public earnings-related programmes, including notional accounts and points schemes as well as traditional defined-benefit plans.

---

* Note that the modeling relates to single, full-career workers drawing the pension from the normal eligibility age. Systems can: *i)* have complex rules for periods out of the labour market (caring for children or in unemployment, for example); *ii)* treat married couples as a single unit; *iii)* adjust benefits for early and late retirement. Since these rules do not affect the modelling under the current assumptions, they are described only briefly.

- DC: defined-contribution, mandatory private plans.

- Occupational: mandatory pensions, which can be provided by employers, industry-wide schemes (Netherlands), profession-based schemes (Sweden) or publicly (Finland, France).

There are some programmes in certain countries that are difficult to classify, including the new savings credit in the United Kingdom, the government's flat-rate contribution to DC plans in Mexico, the end-of-year scheme in Luxembourg and the ATP scheme in Denmark. These are explained in the relevant country studies.

The second row of country charts shows the effect of personal income taxes and social security contributions on relative pension values and replacement rates, giving the gross and net values.

The charts use a standard scale to ease comparisons between countries: the scale for replacement rates runs to 125% while that for relative pension values runs to 2.5 times average earnings. In some cases, pension benefits exceed these maxima and so the measure has been capped at these levels.

The final row of country charts shows, for reference, the taxes and contributions paid by pensioners and workers. This illustrates the source of any concessions to older people in these systems since the values are shown for workers and pensioners *with the same income*. The effect of taxes and contributions on net replacement rates is more complex than illustrated here. Since replacement rates are usually less than 100%, the normal progressivity of the tax system means that people tend to pay fewer taxes when retired regardless of any concessions.

The final row also shows the sources of the net replacement rate. In addition to the components of the pension system shown in the first two charts, this includes the effect of taxes and contributions. This is computed using the results of the tax models on the amount of taxes paid on earnings of a particular level and the amount of taxes due on the pension entitlement calculated for someone earning at that level.

Finally, after the country studies is a short summary of the issues in modelling voluntary occupational pensions. This is followed by brief country-specific studies of Canada, Denmark, the United Kingdom and the United States.

ISBN 92-64-01871-9
Pensions at a Glance
Public Policies across OECD Countries
© OECD 2005

Australia

Australia's pension system has two components: a means-tested age pension plus the superannuation guarantee, a compulsory contribution to a private pension plan. These plans are mainly defined contribution.

Qualifying conditions

The age pension is paid from age 65 for men. Women's pensionable age – currently 62½ – will increase gradually to become 65 from 2013. The minimum age for withdrawing superannuation guarantee benefits is currently 55, but this will increase gradually to 60 by 2025.

Benefit formula

Defined contribution

The superannuation guarantee was introduced in 1992. It consists of a mandatory employer contribution to a private pension plan, which can be an industry-wide fund or a scheme operated by financial-services companies on the employer's behalf. The mandatory contribution rate has been 9% since the 2002-03 tax year.

Employers need not contribute for workers earning less than AUD 450 in a month (equivalent to AUD 5 400 a year or about 12% of average earnings). But they can choose to contribute for these workers. (Note that this floor has not been up-rated in the past.) There is also a limit to the earnings covered by the superannuation guarantee: employers need not contribute for employees' pay above this threshold. For calendar 2002, this limit was AUD 113 460 (calculated from a quarterly limit of AUD 27 510 for 2001-02 and AUD 29 220 for 2002-03). This limit – worth around 2½ times average earnings – is indexed to earnings.

The withdrawal stage of the superannuation guarantee complicates the calculations. Although there are some defined-benefit occupational plans, most employees are members of defined-contribution plans. Members can take out the accumulated capital as a lump sum or some sort of income stream. Currently, most benefits are taken as a lump sum and phased withdrawals are the most popular form of income stream. For comparison with other countries (where defined-benefit plans predominate), the capital from the superannuation guarantee is converted to a price-indexed annuity. The annuity calculation is based on mortality data for Australia. Finally, the calculation is complicated by the tax treatment, described below.

Targeted

The value of the age pension is adjusted biannually. The age pension is paid fortnightly: from September 2001, the single rate of pension was AUD 411, increasing to AUD 422 in

Pension modelling results: Australia

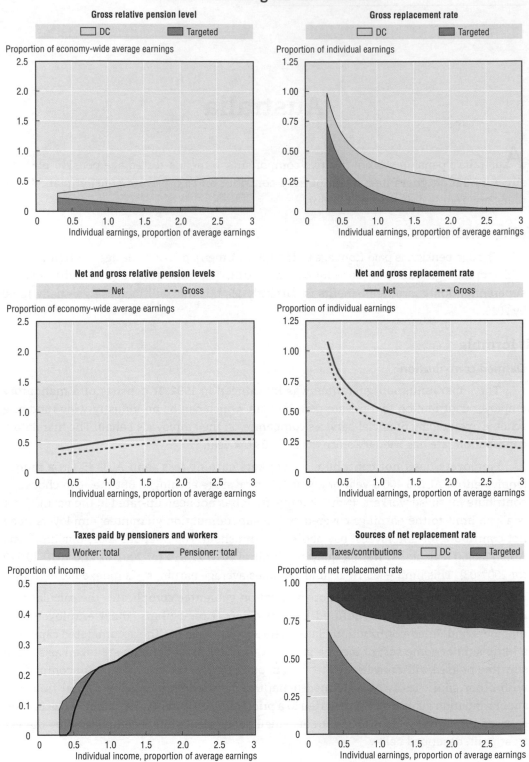

Source: OECD, based on information provided by the countries.

March 2002 and AUD 429 in September 2002. (All values have been rounded to the nearest dollar.) This gives an average for the calendar year of an annual benefit of AUD 10 984, equivalent to around a quarter of average earnings.

The age pension is withdrawn once annual income from other sources exceeds a threshold known as the "free area". This is adjusted annually in July. The values for 2002 were AUD 112 in the first half and AUD 116 in the second half of the year (again calculated fortnightly). The calendar year figure for 2002 was therefore AUD 2 964, or around 7% of average earnings. The withdrawal rate is 40%. There is also an assets test. However, over 90% of pensioners affected have their benefits reduced by the income rather than the assets test (and so it has been assumed in the modelling that the income test is binding). Around a third of pensioners have their benefit reduced by the means test, with the other two-thirds on the full age pension.

The age pension's value is increased in line with prices, but where necessary a special further increase is made to ensure that it does not fall below 25% of pre-tax male total average weekly earnings on the national definition (which is slightly different from the average production worker's earnings used for all countries in OECD analysis).

Personal income tax and social security contributions

Taxation of pensioners

Older Australians are entitled to two personal tax concessions in addition to the standard reliefs.

A credit (the senior Australians tax offset) is available for those of pensionable age (see under qualifying conditions above) who also satisfy a residency test. This is AUD 2 230 for singles in 2002 with income up to an income threshold of AUD 20 000 and is withdrawn at a rate of 12.5% for income in excess of the threshold. The credit is therefore fully withdrawn for incomes of AUD 37 840 and above.

There is a credit for pensioners in receipt of certain pension income (the pensioner tax offset) which has different eligibility criteria from the senior Australians tax offset. It is not possible to claim both of these offsets and the former is more generous for those eligible for both.

The effect of the credit is that all those receiving the full rate of the government pension will have no net income tax liability, and most of those who receive a part pension will have a reduced liability. The credit is non-refundable; it cannot create a negative tax liability.

Taxpayers eligible for the senior Australians tax offset benefit from a higher value of the low-income Medicare levy threshold (AUD 20 500). This means that pensioners receiving the full amount of the offset will pay no Medicare levy. The normal rate of the levy is 1.5% of income.

Taxation of private pensions

The superannuation guarantee has a complex tax treatment, with some tax extracted at all three possible stages: when contributions are made, when investment returns are earned and when benefits are withdrawn.

A 15% tax is levied on employer contributions to the fund. A superannuation surcharge is also applied to contributions for higher-income workers. The rate of the surcharge is determined by the degree to which earnings exceed a threshold. For 2002, the annual average of this threshold was an adjusted taxable income of AUD 87 885 (AUD 85 242 in the first half and AUD 90 527 in the second). For each of a set amount that earnings are above this threshold, the surcharge rate increases by one percentage point. The 2002 average of this amount, known as the "divisor", was AUD 1 257 (AUD 1 219, AUD 1 295 in each half of the year). The maximum surcharge is 15%. The threshold where the superannuation surcharge first applies is worth around 1.9 times average earnings and the full 15% rate applies once earnings reach 2.3 times the average. The superannuation surcharge (for defined-contribution schemes) is imposed on contributions to the superannuation account (and certain transfers into the fund). Although formally paid by the provider, the modelling assumes that this reduces the amount going into the individual pension account.

Investment earnings of the superannuation fund are taxed, again at 15%. (However, the effective tax rate may be lower through imputation credits and the capital-gains-tax discount.)

Benefits are taxable at normal rates on withdrawal, but subject to a 15% rebate. (However, the first AUD 1 000 does not attract a rebate.) The rebate is also subject to a "reasonable benefit limit". For 2003, this lifetime limit was generally AUD 562 195. There is a higher limit for people withdrawing at least half of benefits as an annuity that meets certain conditions. This higher limit is around twice the level of the first: AUD 1 124 384 in 2003. These ceilings are indexed to earnings. The proportion of the pension attracting the rebate is the proportion of the total within the reasonable benefit limit.

The reasonable benefit limit has not been modelled. The modelling gives the accumulated balance in the superannuation fund as around AUD 630 000 at the time of retirement for people earning the maximum amount on which employers must contribute. The assumption that benefits are withdrawn as a price-indexed annuity means that this is below the reasonable benefit threshold.

Social security contributions paid by pensioners

There are no social security contributions in Australia. The age pension and other benefits are financed from general revenues.

Pension modelling results: Australia

Men	Individual earnings, multiple of average					
Women (where different)	0.5	0.75	1	1.5	2	2.5
Gross pension level	32.5	36.3	40.0	47.5	52.4	54.7
(% of average earnings)						
Net pension level	42.6	47.5	52.4	59.2	62.3	64.0
(% of average net earnings)						
Gross replacement rate	65.1	48.4	40.0	31.7	26.2	21.9
(% of individual earnings)						
Net replacement rate	77.0	61.2	52.4	43.1	36.5	31.3
(% of individual net earnings)						
Gross pension wealth	5.7	6.2	6.7	7.7	8.3	8.6
(multiple of average earnings)	6.7	7.2	7.8	8.9	9.6	10.0
Net pension wealth	7.5	8.1	8.8	9.6	9.9	10.1
(multiple of average net earnings)	8.8	9.5	10.2	11.1	11.5	11.7

Austria

A defined-benefit public scheme with an income-tested top-up for low-income pensioners.

Qualifying conditions

Normal pension age is 65 for men and 60 for women. There is a coverage condition: 180 months (15 years) in the last 30 years or 300 months (25 years) during the full lifetime. Alternatively, 180 months of contributions actually paid (as opposed to coverage alone) are sufficient. Insured months are either contributory months (from employment or voluntary contributions) or supplementary (*i.e.*, credited months, known as *Ersatzzeiten*) for which only limited contributions are paid.

Benefit calculation

Earnings-related

The pension benefit currently accrues at 2% of earnings for each year of contributions but this will fall gradually, reaching 1.78% by 2009.

The earnings measure is currently the best 15 years' earnings. The valorisation procedure is complex although in practice adjustments have been closer to price inflation than to earnings growth. The averaging period is being extended; it will reach 40 years from 2028. Valorisation under this new procedure is still under discussion. The modelling takes this full-career measure and assumes that earlier years' earnings are revalued in line with earnings growth.

Contributions are payable up to a ceiling of EUR 39 240, around 175% of average earnings.

In recent years, pensions in payment were adjusted in line with prices up to the average pension; pensions above this threshold were increased by a flat amount, which was equal to the absolute increase given to the average pensioner. This method was used *ad hoc* but it is not legally determined. Thus, adjustment of pensions in payment is discretionary. For the pension wealth calculations, the modelling assumes all pensions are price-indexed.

Targeted

There is a means-tested top-up (*Ausgleichszulage*) that ensures a minimum retirement income of EUR 631 per month for single people and EUR 900 for a couple. There are fourteen annual payments. Again, adjustment of the safety-net income is discretionary; the modelling implicitly assumes that it will rise in line with average earnings.

Pension modelling results: Austria

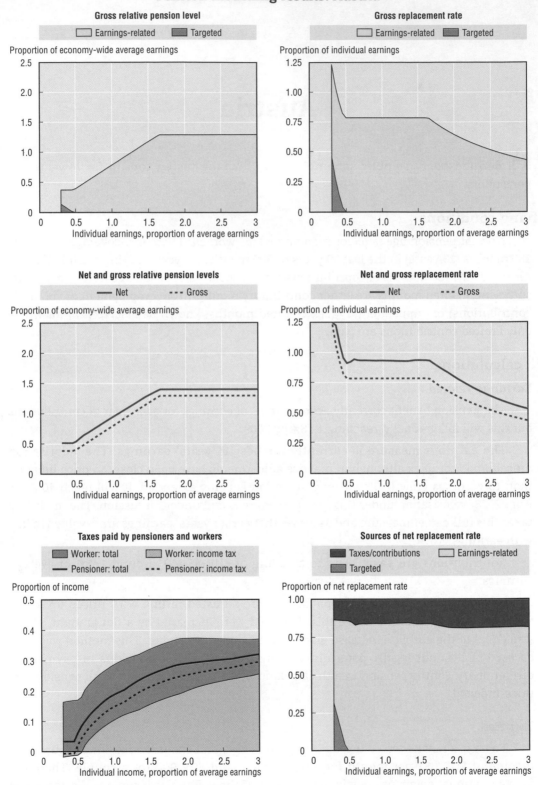

Source: OECD, based on information provided by the countries.

Personal income tax and social security contributions

Taxation of pensioners

There are no special rules for pensioners. Pensioners are unable to claim work expenses if their only income is a pension.

Taxation of pension income

There are no special reliefs for pension income.

Social security contributions paid by pensioners

Pensioners do not pay most social security contributions but do pay for sickness insurance.

Pension modelling results: Austria

Men Women (where different)	Individual earnings, multiple of average					
	0.5	0.75	1	1.5	2	2.5
Gross pension level	39.2	58.7	78.3	117.5	128.7	128.7
(% of average earnings)	*37.0*	*52.1*	*69.4*	*104.1*	*114.1*	*114.1*
Net pension level	52.9	74.2	93.2	130.1	139.3	139.3
(% of average net earnings)	*50.0*	*67.4*	*84.6*	*117.7*	*127.3*	*127.3*
Gross replacement rate	78.3	78.3	78.3	78.3	64.3	51.5
(% of individual earnings)	*74.0*	*69.4*	*69.4*	*69.4*	*57.0*	*45.6*
Net replacement rate	91.2	93.4	93.2	93.5	79.3	63.2
(% of individual net earnings)	*86.1*	*84.8*	*84.6*	*84.6*	*72.5*	*57.8*
Gross pension wealth	6.0	9.0	11.9	17.9	19.6	19.6
(multiple of average earnings)	*7.6*	*10.7*	*14.2*	*21.4*	*23.4*	*23.4*
Net pension wealth	8.1	11.3	14.2	19.8	21.2	21.2
(multiple of average net earnings)	*10.3*	*13.8*	*17.4*	*24.1*	*26.1*	*26.1*

Belgium

An earnings-related public scheme with a minimum pension and a means-tested safety net.

Qualifying conditions

With 30 years' contributions, the pension can be claimed at 60 under the 2002 rules. This contribution condition will increase to 32 years in 2004 and 35 years from 2005. Since a full-career worker from age 20 will meet this condition, the modelling assumes that people draw the pension from age 60.

Normal pensionable age is 65 for men. For women, the eligibility age in 2002 was 62. It will increase to 63 in 2003, to 64 in 2006 and 65 in 2009.

Benefit calculation

Earnings-related

The full replacement rate for a single pensioner is 60% and for those with a dependent spouse, 75%. The earnings measure is average lifetime pay. Earlier years' earnings are revalued in line with prices. Thus, replacement rates on the measure used in the modelling are lower than this target level due to real earnings growth over the career.

The full replacement rate is paid provided the qualifying conditions above are met. For shorter contribution histories, the pension is proportionally reduced.

There is a ceiling to pensionable earnings of EUR 39 368 for 2002 (around 125% of average earnings). This ceiling was frozen in nominal terms between 1982 and 1999.

Pensions in payment are uprated in line with a consumer price index (that excludes some goods). There have also been discretionary real increases (called "adaptations to well-being"). However, these increments have recently been very limited (either to the lowest or the longest-running pensions).

Minimum

There is a minimum annual credit designed to increase pension entitlements for people with low earnings and/or in part-time work. Annual earnings of less than EUR 13 956 (equivalent to around 45% of average earnings) are inflated to this level. To qualify for the minimum credits, at least 15 years' insurance is necessary. (This gives an effective minimum pension for a full-career worker of EUR 11 495 for a single person, worth 37% of average earnings.)

There is also a minimum earnings-related pension of EUR 9 438 for a single person (EUR 11 794 with a dependent spouse) meeting the full contribution condition. For a single person, this is around 30% of average earnings. The benefit value can be reduced

Pension modelling results: Belgium

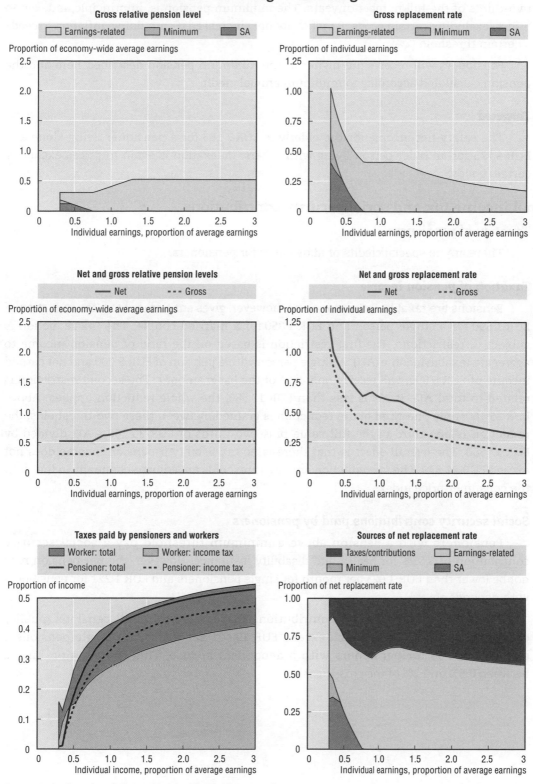

proportionally for less-than-full careers, but only if the beneficiary has a minimum of two-thirds of the full number of years. The minimum pension is, in principle, indexed to prices, excluding certain goods. Benefits are only increased if cumulative inflation exceeds a certain threshold (2%).

Pensioners will receive the higher of the minimum pension described here and the pension calculated according to minimum annual credit.

Targeted

The safety-net income for the elderly is EUR 7 163 for a pensioner living alone and EUR 4 775 for an older person living with others. Indexation is again to prices excluding certain goods.

Personal income tax and social security contributions

Taxation of pensioners

There are no special credits or allowances for pensioners.

Taxation of pension income

Pensions are taxable. Pension income, however, gives entitlement to a tax reduction of EUR 1 590 for a single person and EUR 1 850 for a married couple. The tax reduction is subject to restrictions. The first restriction is based on the ratio of pension income to aggregate taxable income (ATI). A single person with a pension of EUR 5 000 and net earned income of EUR 5 000, will receive only half of the basic amount. The second restriction is related to total ATI. If ATI is less than EUR 17 580, the whole reduction applies. Above EUR 35 160, only one-third of the reduction is granted. Between these two thresholds, the reduction is one-third of the full value plus two-thirds of EUR 35 160 – ATI divided by EUR 17 580. The overall effect is that there is no tax liability if pension income does not exceed EUR 11 849. The tax reduction and the thresholds are adjusted annually in line with the consumer price index.

Social security contributions paid by pensioners

Pensioners with a pension above a minimum threshold pay a social security contribution of 3.55% for health and disability insurance. However, the net pension may not be lower than EUR 1 023 per month for single pensioners and EUR 1 221 for pensioners with dependents.

There are also "solidarity" contributions that are levied on all pensions (public, occupational and private) which exceed EUR 13 401 per annum for single pensioners and EUR 16 751 for pensioners with a dependent spouse. This contribution ranges between 0.5% and 2% of the gross pension.

Pension modelling results: Belgium

Men	Individual earnings, multiple of average					
Women (where different)	0.5	0.75	1	1.5	2	2.5
Gross pension level	30.8	30.8	37.3	47.9	47.9	47.9
(% of average earnings)						
Net pension level	52.1	52.1	62.8	68.4	68.4	68.4
(% of average net earnings)						
Gross replacement rate	61.6	41.1	37.3	31.9	23.9	19.2
(% of individual earnings)						
Net replacement rate	82.7	63.8	62.8	50.6	40.6	34.2
(% of individual net earnings)						
Gross pension wealth	5.5	5.5	7.3	9.4	9.4	9.4
(multiple of average earnings)	*6.3*	*6.3*	*8.4*	*10.7*	*10.7*	*10.7*
Net pension wealth	9.3	9.3	11.3	12.9	12.9	12.9
(multiple of average net earnings)	*10.7*	*10.7*	*12.9*	*14.8*	*14.8*	*14.8*

Canada

A universal, flat-rate pension, known as old-age security, can be topped up with an income-tested benefit, known as the guaranteed income supplement. A tier of earnings-related benefits is known as the Canada Pension Plan/Québec Pension Plan. These two plans offer broadly similar benefits.

Qualifying conditions

The basic pension is subject to a residency test, with $^{1}/_{40}$th of the maximum pension earned for each year of residence after age 18 up to a maximum of 40 years. A minimum of ten years' residency is required to receive any benefit. It is payable from age 65.

For the earnings-related scheme, a full pension requires 40 years' contributions but a single year's contribution is sufficient to generate an entitlement. Normal pension age is again 65 but an early pension can be claimed from age 60.

Benefit calculation

Basic

The average 2002 benefit level of old-age security was CAD 5 320, equivalent to 14% of average earnings. The value of the basic pension is price-indexed.

This pension is subject to an income test operated through the tax system (a "claw-back"). Once income exceeds CAD 56 968, the basic pension is withdrawn at a 15% rate. This threshold is equivalent to just under 1½ times average earnings. It is also indexed to prices.

Targeted

The guaranteed income supplement gives a maximum pension, including the universal (basic) benefit, which averaged CAD 11 600 in 2002 (30% of average earnings) for a single person.

This is withdrawn against income other than the basic pension at a 50% rate. The target benefit level is price-indexed.

Earnings-related

This scheme targets a 25% replacement rate based on average lifetime salary, with earlier years' pay revalued in line with economy-wide earnings. As noted previously, the full benefit requires 40 years' contributions with proportional reductions for shorter work histories. The maximum earnings-related pension for 2002 was CAD 779 a month (just under a quarter of average earnings).

Pension modelling results: Canada

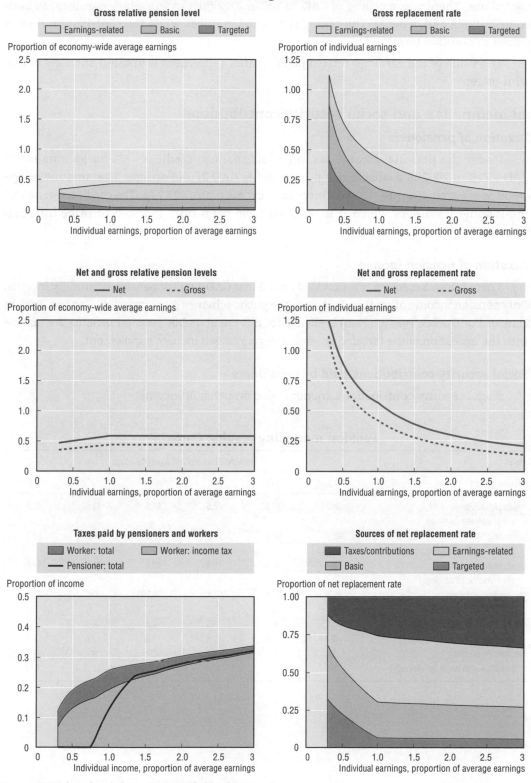

Source: OECD, based on information provided by the countries.

People earning less than CAD 3 500 a year (10% of average earnings) are not required to contribute. There was a ceiling of CAD 39 100 in 2002 (just over average earnings) to both contributions and benefits. The ceiling is indexed to prices while the contribution floor is frozen in nominal terms.

The value of the earnings-related pension after retirement is uprated annually in line with prices.

Personal income tax and social security contributions

Taxation of pensioners

Under the personal income tax, an additional age credit of 16% on an amount of CAD 3 728 in 2002 is available if total income is CAD 27 749 or less. The amount of age credit is reduced at a rate of 15% of income in excess of CAD 27 749. The credit amount and the income level over which it is reduced have been fully indexed to price inflation since 2000.

Taxation of pension income

There is also a credit of 16% provided on the first CAD 1 000 of pension or annuity income. Only pension income other than that from the public schemes (basic pension, Canada Pension Plan and/or Québec Pension Plan) is eligible for this credit. Public pension benefits are taxable with the exception of the targeted scheme, the guaranteed income supplement.

Social security contributions paid by pensioners

Social security contributions are not levied on pension income.

Pension modelling results: Canada

Men	Individual earnings, multiple of average					
Women (where different)	0.5	0.75	1	1.5	2	2.5
Gross pension level	36.2	39.3	42.5	42.5	42.5	42.5
(% of average earnings)						
Net pension level	48.7	52.9	57.1	57.2	57.2	57.2
(% of average net earnings)						
Gross replacement rate	72.4	52.4	42.5	28.4	21.3	17.0
(% of individual earnings)						
Net replacement rate	89.4	67.6	57.1	39.5	30.6	25.1
(% of individual net earnings)						
Gross pension wealth	5.5	6.0	6.5	6.5	6.5	6.5
(multiple of average earnings)	*6.4*	*7.0*	*7.6*	*7.6*	*7.6*	*7.6*
Net pension wealth	7.4	8.1	8.7	8.7	8.7	8.7
(multiple of average net earnings)	*8.7*	*9.4*	*10.2*	*10.2*	*10.2*	*10.2*

Czech Republic

The public scheme has a basic element and an earnings-related part calculated according to a progressive formula. There is also a minimum pension in this programme.

Qualifying conditions

A phased increase in the standard retirement age will take it to 63 for men from 2013. The pension eligibility age will be 59-63 for women depending on the number of children that they have. A full pension requires 25 years' coverage but people with 15 years' contributions can receive a pension from 65.

Benefit calculation

Basic

The value of the basic pension is CZK 1 310 per month. There is no statutory indexation requirement for the value of the basic benefit alone. However, total pensions in payment must be increased by at least prices plus one third of real wage growth (see below).

Earnings-related

The earnings-related pension gives 1.5% of earnings for each year of contributions. The earnings measure currently averages across all years since 1985, but it will gradually reach 30 years. There is a progressive formula, with the first CZK 7 100 per month replaced at 100%, the slice of earnings between this limit and CZK 16 800 at 30% with 10% replacement above this level. The first threshold, below which there is 100% replacement, is equivalent to just over 40% of average earnings, while the second threshold is just below average earnings. There is no statutory indexation requirement for these thresholds. Earlier years' earnings in the benefit formula are valorised fully to average earnings.

There is no specific statutory indexation requirement for the earnings-related pension component in payment. However, the combined total pension benefit (flat-rate and earnings-related components) is adjusted at least to price inflation with additional, real increases of at least one third of real wage growth.

Minimum

The total value of the minimum pension benefit is CZK 2 080, which is made up of a minimum earnings-related pension of CZK 770 plus the basic component of CZK 1 310. This combined minimum pension is indexed in the same way as described above.

Pension modelling results: Czech Republic

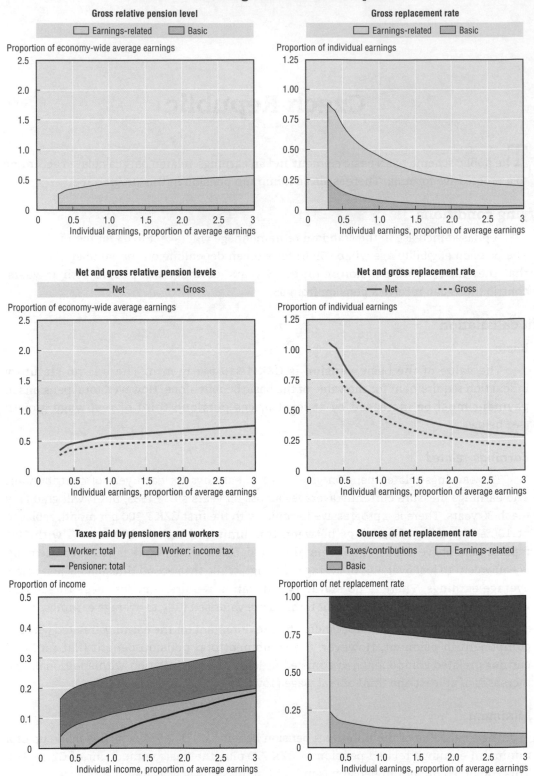

Source: OECD, based on information provided by the countries.

Social assistance

Older people are covered by the general social-assistance scheme and related benefits in kind. The target safety-net income for a single-person household is CZK 1 780.

Personal income tax and social security contributions

Taxation of pensioners

Old-age pensions are not taxed up to a value of CZK 144 000. The standard tax-free allowance is CZK 38 400, giving pensioners an effective allowance four times higher than workers have.

Taxation of pensions

There are no special reliefs for pension income.

Social security contributions paid by pensioners

Recipients of old age pensions do not pay social security contributions.

Pension modelling results: Czech Republic

Men	Individual earnings, multiple of average					
Women (where different)	0.5	0.75	1	1.5	2	2.5
Gross pension level	35.3	40.0	44.4	47.6	50.7	53.9
(% of average earnings)						
Net pension level	46.2	52.4	58.2	62.3	66.4	70.6
(% of average net earnings)						
Gross replacement rate	70.5	53.3	44.4	31.7	25.4	21.6
(% of individual earnings)						
Net replacement rate	88.3	68.3	58.2	42.9	35.3	31.0
(% of individual net earnings)						
Gross pension wealth	5.8	6.6	7.3	7.8	8.3	8.9
(multiple of average earnings)	6.8	7.7	8.6	9.2	9.8	10.4
Net pension wealth	7.6	8.6	9.6	10.2	10.9	11.6
(multiple of average net earnings)	8.9	10.1	11.3	12.1	12.9	13.7

Denmark

There is a public basic scheme with an income-tested supplement for low-income pensioners. There are also two schemes based on individuals' contribution records, the ATP and SP, or special pension savings schemes. In addition, voluntary occupational schemes cover about 80% of the workforce.

Qualifying conditions

The normal pension age is 65 (67 for people born before 1 July 1939). A full state old-age pension requires 40 years' residence. Shorter periods qualify for a pro-rated benefit (subject to a minimum of three years' residence). A full entitlement under the labour-market supplementary pension (ATP) and the special saving scheme (SP) requires a full career of contributions. The ATP scheme was established in 1964 and a full career is considered as full-time contributions at the normal rate since this date.

Benefit calculation

Basic

The full amount is DKK 4 377 per month or DKK 52 524 per year, equivalent to 17% of average earnings. There is an earnings test which means that the benefit will be reduced if pay exceeds DKK 223 200 per year (around three-quarters of average earnings). The benefit is withdrawn at a rate of 30% against earnings above this level. (The indexation of the basic pension amount is described below.)

Targeted

The full pension supplement is DKK 4 406 per month or DKK 52 872 per year for single persons (again, around 17% of average earnings). The amounts are tested against all sources of income (including ATP, SP and voluntary occupational pensions) apart from the basic pension amount. The pension supplement is withdrawn once income exceeds DKK 49 200 a year for single persons (around 16% of average earnings). The withdrawal rate is 30% of income above the threshold for a single person.

The basic amount and the pension supplement are uprated annually in line with average earnings. If nominal earnings growth exceeds 2% a year (measured over the previous two years), a maximum of 0.3 percentage points of the excess of earnings growth over 2% is allocated to a social-spending reserve. The baseline economic assumptions are that nominal wage growth is above 2%, and so the maximum allocation to the reserve is taken into account in the modelling.

Pension modelling results: Denmark

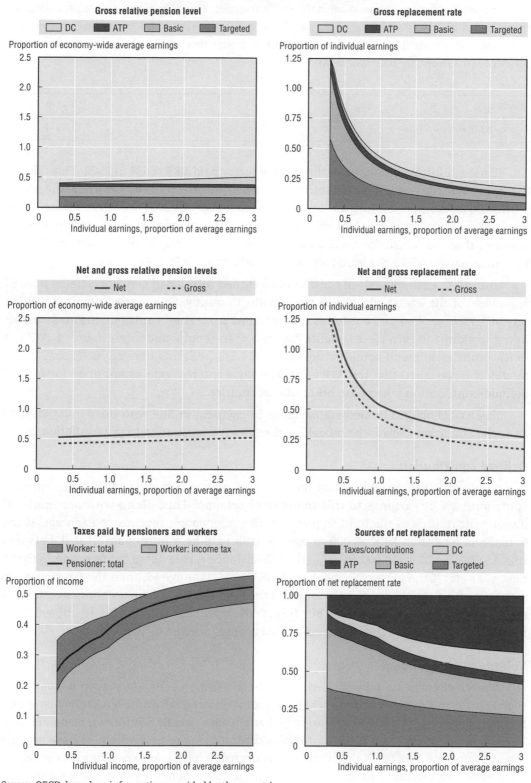

ATP scheme

The ATP scheme is based on deferred annuities. Contributions are split with two-thirds paid by the employer and one-third by the worker. The contribution amount depends not on earnings but on the number of hours worked as shown in the following schedule (for monthly paid workers):

Monthly hours	< 39	39-77	78-116	> 116
Contribution, DKK/month	0	74.55	149.10	223.65

Thus, a full-time employee in the private sector paid DKK 2 684 in 2002. The value of the contribution is adjusted sporadically based on negotiations between the social partners. For example, an increase of 9% has been agreed for 2006. However, this will only partially make up for earlier lags behind the increase in average earnings. The modelling assumes that the contribution will increase in line with average earnings, which has been the broad pattern since the introduction of the ATP scheme in 1964.

Until 2002, each DKK 396 of contributions earned DKK 100 of pension benefits from 67 regardless of the age at which they were made. Currently, an assumed nominal interest rate of 1.5% is applied to the value of contributions paid. Thus, contributions made earlier in the working life earn more benefits (because of the compound interest effect). ATP is a "with-profit" scheme: if actual returns exceed 1.5%, pensions may be increased. In the model, it is assumed that the ATP earns the same interest rate as assumed for funded defined-contribution schemes in other OECD countries.

The ATP is obliged to increase pensions in payment in line with price inflation if its financial condition allows. The modelling assumes full indexation to price inflation.

Defined contribution

Employees, self-employed and recipients of unemployment and sickness benefits contribute 1% of earnings to this mandatory scheme. This, along with accumulated investment returns of the fund, is paid out after the worker reaches pension age. If the balance is less than DKK 15 000 at age 65, it is paid as a lump sum. If it is between DKK 15 000 and DKK 120 000, then $1/_{10}$th of the balance is paid out in the first year, $1/_9$th the next year etc. If the balance is more than DKK 120 000 at age 65, then the payments are monthly with annual adjustments to reflect the market value of the account. Investments are currently managed centrally. But from 2005, members will be able to choose their manager and portfolio. There is no ceiling to earnings covered by this scheme.

Voluntary occupational

These schemes are fully funded defined-contribution schemes agreed between the social partners. Coverage of these schemes is almost universal. Contributions schemes are typically between 9% and 17% of earnings. Benefits are usually withdrawn as an annuity. The assumed interest rate is 1.5% for recent contributions or new schemes. However, the schemes operate on a "with-profit" basis, with pension increases depending on the return on assets and mortality experience of the fund. Many schemes also allow lump sum withdrawals. From 2000, the annuitisation calculation must use unisex mortality tables.

Targeted cash benefits and services

There are special needs- and income-tested benefits for over 65s. In addition to free health and long-term care, favourable housing benefit rules, heating allowances and other benefits are available.

Personal income taxes and social security contributions

Taxation of pensioners

There are no special tax allowances or credits for pensioners.

Taxation of pension income

Pension payments are subject to income tax. There are no special reliefs for pension income.

The payment under a funded pension scheme is subject to a tax of 40% on lump-sum withdrawals. Since 1984, the return on assets in pension schemes has been subject to a special tax. From 1984 to mid-1998, bonds were taxed at a variable rate. The rate depended on the interest rate and inflation (*i.e.*, real-interest tax). The rate ranged between 40 and 50% for most of the period. From mid-1998, the return on equities was taxed at 5%. In 2000, the tax was changed to a fixed rate of 26% on bond returns and 5% on equities. Since 2001, the rate has been 15% for all types of investment income. This tax regime applies to both the SP and to occupational plans.

Social security contributions paid by pensioners

Pensioners do not pay social security contributions.

Pension modelling results: Denmark

Men	Individual earnings, multiple of average					
Women (where different)	0.5	0.75	1	1.5	2	2.5
Gross pension level	41.2	42.3	43.3	45.4	47.5	49.6
(% of average earnings)						
Net pension level	51.9	53.0	54.1	56.4	58.7	60.9
(% of average net earnings)						
Gross replacement rate	82.4	56.4	43.3	30.3	23.8	19.8
(% of individual earnings)						
Net replacement rate	95.6	68.0	54.1	42.5	35.5	30.8
(% of individual net earnings)						
Gross pension wealth	7.0	7.2	7.4	7.7	8.0	8.3
(multiple of average earnings)	*8.1*	*8.2*	*8.4*	*8.7*	*9.0*	*9.3*
Net pension wealth	7.5	7.7	7.8	8.2	8.5	8.8
(multiple of average net earnings)	*10.2*	*10.3*	*10.5*	*10.8*	*11.2*	*11.5*

Finland

The two-tier pension system consists of a basic state pension, which is pension-income-tested, and a range of statutory earnings-related schemes, with very similar rules for different groups. The schemes for private-sector employees are partially pre-funded while the public-sector schemes are pay-as-you-go financed (with buffer funds to even out future increases in pension contributions).

Qualifying conditions

The national pension is subject to a residency test (but no contribution requirements), withdrawn against pension income from the earnings-related schemes. Both the national and the earnings-related pensions are payable from age 65. The full benefit is payable with 40 years residence as an adult, with *pro rata* adjustments for shorter periods of residence.

Benefit calculation

Earnings-related

From 2005, the accrual rate will be 1.5% of pensionable pay at ages 18-52, 1.9% at ages 53-62 and 4.5% at ages 63-67. Currently, the accrual rates are 1.5% at younger ages and 2.5% between ages 60 and 64. The modelling includes the effect of this reform. For a full-career worker working from age 20 until retirement at age 65, the total lifetime accrual will be 77.5% of pensionable earnings. Currently, there is a maximum replacement rate of 60% of pensionable earnings but this is abolished from 2005.

Currently, earnings are averaged over the last ten years of employment in a particular scheme. Years with exceptionally low earnings can be ignored (to a maximum of one third of total years of coverage). From 2005 onwards, pensionable pay will be based on average earnings of the whole career. Earlier years' earnings are re-valued in line with a mix of economy-wide earnings and prices. Currently, wage and price inflation are equally weighted but from 2005 onwards, wage growth will have an 80% weight and price inflation, 20%. At the baseline assumptions for prices and wages growth, this policy reduces the value of the pension to 91.5% compared with a policy of full earnings valorisation of earlier years' pay.

There is no contribution floor and no ceiling to contributions or pensionable earnings. Pensionable pay is defined as gross earnings less employees' pension contributions (which are described below). Note, however, that the replacement rates are shown relative to total gross earnings (for comparison with other countries) rather than this measure of pensionable pay.

After retirement, the earnings-related pension is uprated using a formula of 20% of earnings inflation and 80% of price inflation. Under current rules, pensions drawn early (before the age of 65) have a more generous indexation procedure: 50% of earnings inflation

Pension modelling results: Finland

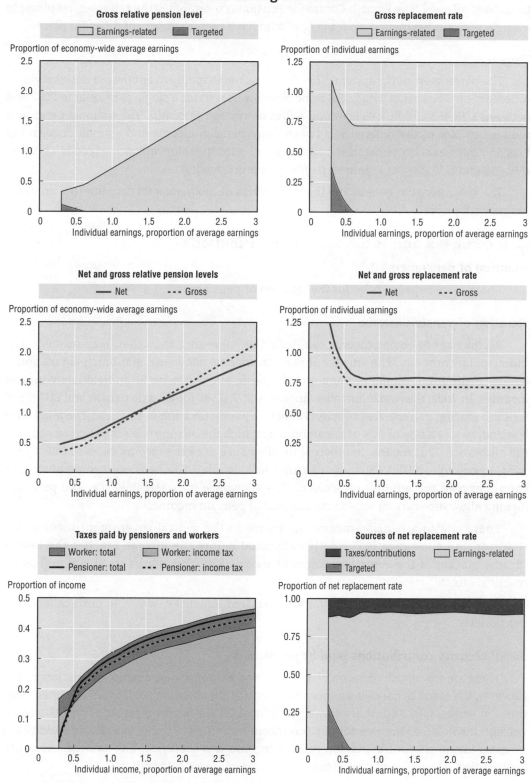

Source: OECD, based on information provided by the countries.

and 50% of price inflation. From 2005 onwards, however, 20% earnings and 80% prices will be used at all ages. The Finnish Centre for Pensions co-ordinates the schemes, resulting in a single pension payment even for people who have been members of different plans.

Targeted

The parameters of the system differ from one municipality to another to reflect regional differences in the cost of living. The basic monthly benefit for a single pensioner in 2002 was between EUR 467 and EUR 488 (around a fifth of average earnings). The national pension is reduced by 50% of the difference between other pension income and a small disregard of EUR 550 per year. No pension is payable once other pension income exceeds between EUR 958 and EUR 999 per month (depending on municipality).

The basic pension benefit and the parameters of the means test are uprated annually in line with prices.

Personal income tax and social security contributions

Taxation of pensioners

There are no special rules for the taxation of pensioners.

Taxation of pension income

Recipients of pension income can deduct an allowance from their income subject to municipal income tax. The amount of pension-income allowance in municipal taxation is based on the full national pension and the basic allowance for all individuals with low incomes. In 2002, the maximum allowance was EUR 6 540 for a single person and EUR 5 580 for each partner in a married couple. (There is separate taxation of couples.) The allowance is withdrawn at a rate of 70% of the amount by which the income subject to tax exceeds the full allowance. This means that there is no allowance once the income exceeds EUR 15 883 (single person) or EUR 13 552 (each partner in a couple). The pension-income allowance cannot exceed the amount of pension. The allowance is "wasteable": i.e., the pension-income allowance cannot exceed the amount of pension income.

There is also a pension-income allowance in the central-government income tax. However, the allowance is currently exhausted before the income reaches the lowest income bracket of the central-government income tax. This allowance therefore has no practical effect.

Workers receive a deduction for work-related expenses, which is not available for pensioners.

Social security contributions paid by pensioners

There are no contributions on pension income for pension or unemployment insurance. However, the same sickness insurance contributions are levied on pensioners' incomes as on those of workers. In 2002, there was an additional 0.4% sickness insurance contribution on pension income (i.e., the rate for pension income was 1.5% + 0.4%). In 2003, this additional sickness-insurance contribution on pension income was abolished. The sickness-insurance contribution is levied on taxable income as defined in municipal taxation.

Pension modelling results: Finland

Men	Individual earnings, multiple of average					
Women (where different)	0.5	0.75	1	1.5	2	2.5
Gross pension level	40.0	53.6	71.5	107.2	142.9	178.6
(% of average earnings)						
Net pension level	52.5	63.1	78.8	108.4	135.2	161.7
(% of average net earnings)						
Gross replacement rate	80.0	71.5	71.5	71.5	71.5	71.5
(% of individual earnings)						
Net replacement rate	90.7	78.8	78.8	79.2	78.3	79.3
(% of individual net earnings)						
Gross pension wealth	6.3	8.4	11.2	16.9	22.5	28.1
(multiple of average earnings)	*7.4*	*10.0*	*13.3*	*20.0*	*26.6*	*33.3*
Net pension wealth	8.2	9.9	12.4	17.0	21.3	25.4
(multiple of average net earnings)	*9.7*	*11.8*	*14.7*	*20.2*	*25.2*	*30.1*

France

A two-tier system, with an earnings-related public pension and mandatory occupational schemes, based on a points system. The public scheme also has a minimum pension.

Qualifying conditions

A full state pension will require 40 years' contributions, compared with 37.5 years currently. Normal pension age is 60. The minimum pension has the same qualifying conditions as the public, earnings-related scheme.

Benefit calculation

Earnings-related

The state pension targets a replacement rate of 50% after a full career. For contribution periods less than a full career, the target replacement rate is reduced *pro rata* and by an additional penalty for each years missing (or each year the pension is drawn before 65).

The earnings measure is based on a number of best years of earnings, valorised in line with price inflation. From 2008 onwards, pay will be averaged over 25 years. Currently, it is around 20 years. At the baseline assumptions, the policy of prices valorisation with the best 25 years earnings measure gives a pension value of 79% of that resulting with a policy of full earnings valorisation.

Because of the limited number of years included in the earnings measure for calculating pension benefits and the policy of valorisation in line with prices, the replacement rate in the French public system is very sensitive to the time profile of earnings throughout the worker's career. (This effect is analysed further for several countries in Part I, Annex I.2, Sections 2 and 3.) Given the baseline assumption of continuous real earnings growth of 2% over a worker's career, combined with the fact that the OECD calculations use the lifetime revalued average earnings as reference salary, the replacement rates calculated are lower than those calculated using the observed salary progression in France, where increases are concentrated primarily in the first half of the career. National projections* for the generation born in 1948 whose salaries grow from 80% to 160% of average earnings with earnings growth concentrated in the first 25 years of the career show an average replacement rate of 77%, that is 12 percentage points higher than the OECD's baseline result.

There is a ceiling on eligible earnings, which in 2002 was EUR 28 224, equivalent to around 125% of average earnings.

Benefits in payment are indexed to prices.

---

* Raynaud, E. (2004), "Les retraites de la génération 1948, une illustration par quelques cas-types", *Études et Résultats*, No. 331, Drees, Paris.

Pension modelling results: France

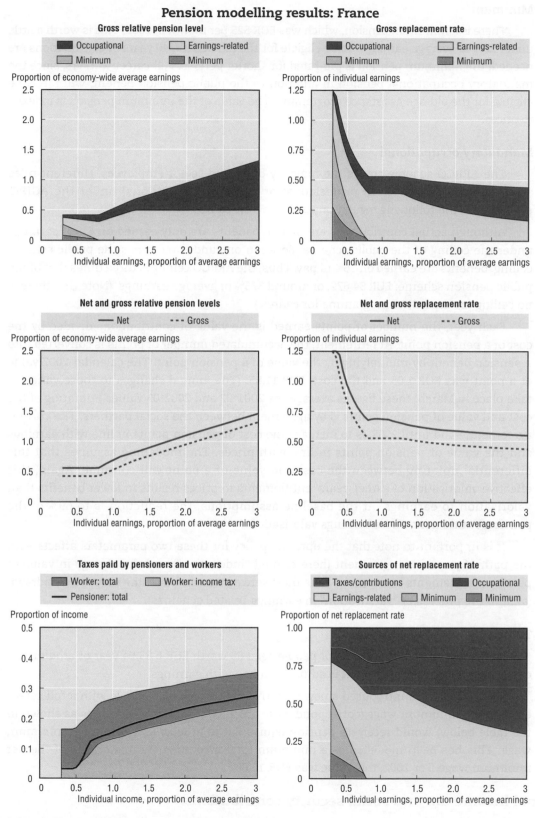

Source: OECD, based on information provided by the countries.

Minimum

There is a minimum pension, which was EUR 525 per month in 2002. This is worth a little under 30% of average earnings. To be eligible for the full benefit, 40 years of contributions are needed; the minimum pension is pro-rated for shorter periods. Full-career workers, since the mandatory occupational pension in addition to the public pension benefit, will rarely be eligible for the old-age assistance programme. The value of the minimum pension is indexed to prices.

Mandatory occupational

The ARRCO scheme covers the majority of private-sector employees. Different rules apply to "cadres" (those in professional or managerial positions) under the AGIRC programme; the following regulations apply to non-cadres.

Although actual contributions are higher, benefits are only earned on 6% of earnings under the ceiling of the public scheme. Between one and three times the public-scheme ceiling, benefits are earned on 16% of pay. Thus, the ARRCO ceiling is three times that of the public pension scheme: EUR 84 672, or around 375% of average earnings. (Note that there is no ceiling for the AGIRC programme for cadres.)

Each year, the number of points earned is the value of contributions divided by the cost of a pension point. At retirement, the accumulated number of points is converted into a pension benefit by multiplying by the value of a pension point. The calendar 2002 value of a point was EUR 1.05 and the cost, EUR 11.85. (The annual changes to these variables take place in March: these figures average the 2001-02 and 2002-03 values.) Uprating of the cost and value of pension points is by agreement between the social partners. The current agreement, valid until 2008, is to increase the cost of pension points in line with earnings and the value of pension points in line with prices. The modelling assumes that this differential uprating between the cost and value of a point will continue. Again, this effective valorisation of earlier years' entitlements to prices results in lower benefits than valorisation to earnings. At the baseline assumptions, the reduction is to 69% of the pension entitlement under earnings valorisation.

It is important to note that the uprating policy for these two parameters affects both the path of pensions in payment (here termed "indexation") and the change in value of pension entitlements between the time they were earned and the time they are withdrawn (akin to the process of "valorisation" in earnings-related schemes).

Targeted

There is a minimum income for people aged 65 worth EUR 6 832 a year or around 30% of average earnings. This benefit is adjusted in line with earnings.

The 2003 reform introduced a new objective that, from 2008, people with a full career earning the minimum wage (corresponding to about 60% of average earnings as shown in the table below) would receive a pension equivalent to at least 85% of the net minimum wage. This has been modelled as a minimum total income guarantee of 85% of the net minimum wage. For 2002, this value was EUR 10 882.

Personal income tax and social security contributions

Taxation of pensioners

There are no specific deductions for older people.

Taxation of pension income

There are no special reliefs.

Social security contributions paid by pensioners

Older people are not liable for standard social security contributions. However, they pay the general social tax (CSG, *contribution sociale généralisée*) of 6%. There is an exemption for the lowest-income pensioners (depending on liability for the personal income tax and the housing tax, *taxe d'habitation*), which means that some 40% of older people do not pay CSG.

Pension modelling results: France

Men	Individual earnings, multiple of average					
Women (where different)	0.6	0.75	1	1.5	2	2.5
Gross pension level	42.1	42.1	49.4	70.9	88.0	105.2
(% of average earnings)						
Net pension level	55.5	55.5	65.0	84.3	102.6	120.1
(% of average net earnings)						
Gross replacement rate	70.1	56.1	49.4	47.3	44.0	42.1
(% of individual earnings)						
Net replacement rate	84.2	70.8	65.0	58.7	55.3	53.4
(% of individual net earnings)						
Gross pension wealth	7.6	7.6	8.9	12.8	15.9	18.9
(multiple of average earnings)	*8.7*	*8.7*	*10.2*	*14.7*	*18.2*	*21.8*
Net pension wealth	10.0	10.0	11.7	15.2	18.5	21.6
(multiple of average net earnings)	*11.5*	*11.5*	*13.5*	*17.5*	*21.3*	*24.9*

Germany

The public pension system has a single tier. It is based on pension points. There is a social-assistance safety net for low-income pensioners.

Qualifying conditions

The pension is payable from age 65 with five years' contributions and from age 63 with 35 years'. Fewer than five years' contributions earn no benefit.

Benefit calculation

Earnings-related

A year's contribution at the average earnings of contributors earns one point. Contributions are levied on monthly earnings between EUR 325 and EUR 4 500 (2002 values). The floor and ceiling are equivalent to 12 and 163% of average earnings respectively. People in short-term employment (up to 50 working days a year) are exempted regardless of their earnings, but people who work 15 hours or more a week must contribute even if their earnings fall below the floor. The ceiling also applies to the number of benefit points earned. Average covered earnings were EUR 28 626 in 2002, equivalent to 86% of the earnings of the average production worker in that year (the measure used here).

The sum of points at pension age is multiplied by a monthly "pension-point value", which was EUR 25.31 in the first half of 2002 and EUR 25.86 in the second half of the year. The first three year's contributions before the age of 25 are adjusted upwards to the lesser of 75% of the individual's total pension entitlement or 75% of his or her lifetime average pay.

The pension-point value is uprated annually in line with gross wages subject to an adjustment for increases in the total (employer and employee) contribution rate to the public scheme. The government aims to limit this rate to 22%. In 2002, the total contribution rate was 19.1%. In the long term, therefore, the pension-point value will fall relative to real earnings.

A further change in rules was legislated in 2004 but it has not been modelled. The "sustainability factor" will link the uprating of the pension-point value to changes in the system dependency ratio, that is, the ratio of pensioners to contributors.

Some of the parameters are slightly different in the new Länder.

Social assistance

The benefit value is determined regionally. The government pays the health and long-term care contributions of older social-assistance recipients. There is also a supplement to cover housing and fuel costs. Average total social-assistance receipt in the Western Länder in 2002 was EUR 648 per month.

Pension modelling results: Germany

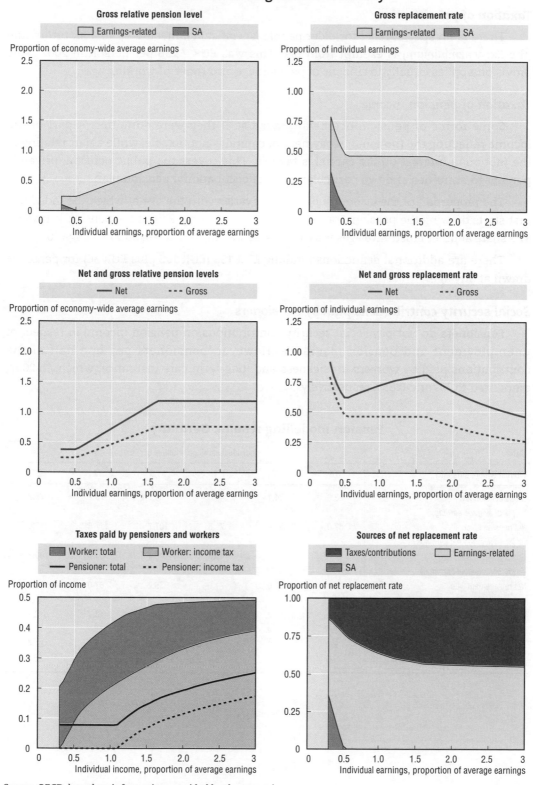

Source: OECD, based on information provided by the countries.

Personal income tax and social security contributions

Taxation of pensioners

There is no special relief for older people (specifically). Income up to a statutory line (the *Existenzminimum*) is exempt from tax. This was EUR 7 236 per person in 2002. This provision applies equally to citizens of pension age and those of working age.

Taxation of pension income

Some forms of pension income are taxed as if they were annuities. A part of the income reflecting the (notional) repayment of capital is not taxable, while a part relating to the (notional) interest on the capital is taxable. This covers the public pension, privately purchased annuities and two particular types of occupational pension plan.

The proportion of the income subject to tax varies with the age at which the individual first starts drawing the pension. For retirement at age 65, only 27% of the pension is taxable. The share at other illustrative ages is as follows: 38% at 55, 32% at 60 and 21% at age 70.

There are additional deductions totalling EUR 138 (EUR 102 plus EUR 36) for pensions drawn at any age.

Social security contributions paid by pensioners

Pensioners do not pay social security contributions on pension income in respect of unemployment and pension insurance. However, pensioners pay one-half of the contributions paid by workers for sickness and long-term care insurance, which, in 2002, amounted to 7% and 0.85% respectively.

Pension modelling results: Germany

Men	Individual earnings, multiple of average					
Women (where different)	0.5	0.75	1	1.5	2	2.5
Gross pension level	23.6	34.4	45.8	68.7	75.2	75.2
(% of average earnings)						
Net pension level	37.0	53.8	71.8	107.7	117.8	117.8
(% of average net earnings)						
Gross replacement rate	47.3	45.8	45.8	45.8	37.6	30.1
(% of individual earnings)						
Net replacement rate	61.7	66.6	71.8	79.2	67.0	54.2
(% of individual net earnings)						
Gross pension wealth	4.3	6.2	8.3	12.5	13.7	13.7
(multiple of average earnings)	*5.1*	*7.4*	*9.8*	*14.8*	*16.2*	*16.2*
Net pension wealth	6.7	9.8	13.0	19.6	21.4	21.4
(multiple of average net earnings)	*8.0*	*11.6*	*15.4*	*23.1*	*25.3*	*25.3*

PENSIONS AT A GLANCE – ISBN 92-64-01871-9 – © OECD 2005

Greece

An earnings-related public scheme with two components plus a series of minimum pensions/social safety nets. The system described applies to labour-market entrants from 1993.

Qualifying conditions

The normal pensionable age is 65 for men and women entering the labour force from 1993. A pension from this age requires a minimum of 4 500 days of contributions (equivalent to 15 years). Workers with a contribution record of 11 100 working days (37 years) can retire on a full benefit regardless of age. There are concessions for people who work in arduous or hazardous occupations and for women with dependant or disabled children.

The minimum pension requires 15 years' contributions.

Benefit formula

Earnings-related scheme: main component

For labour-market entrants from 1993, the pension is 2% of earnings for each year of contributions up to 35 years. The earnings measure is the average over the last five years before retirement. Earlier years' pay is adjusted ("valorised") in line with annual increases defined in national incomes policy.

There is a maximum pension, calculated as four times the 1991 GNP per capita, linked to the evolution of civil servants' pensions. For 2002, this cap on pension benefits was EUR 2 149 per month. The calculations indicate that, for a full-career worker, this is equivalent to a ceiling on pensionable earnings of 325% of average earnings.

Adjustment of pensions in payment is discretionary. In the last five years, pension increases have been progressive with one exception, when all pensions were increased by the same proportion (see below). In 1999-2001, increases of low pensions were substantially larger than price inflation. However, in 2002, they lagged behind. Given the lack of consistent practice in recent benefit adjustments, pension wealth calculations are based on prices indexation.

Pension modelling results: Greece

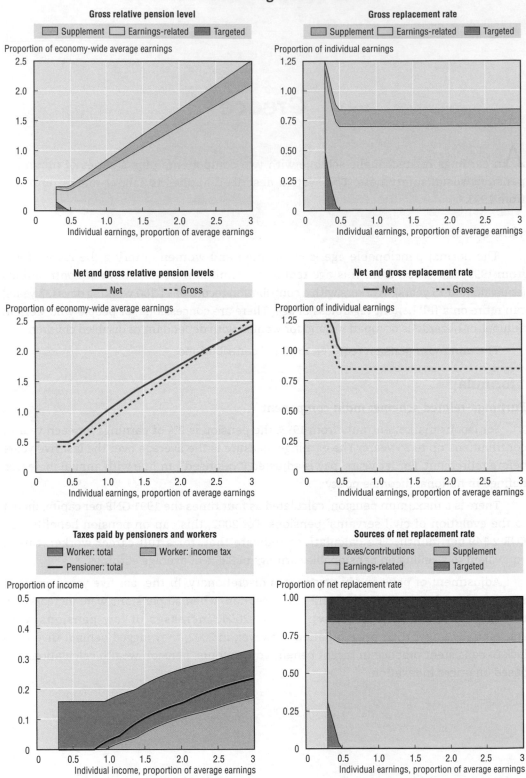

Source: OECD, based on information provided by the countries.

	1999	2000	2001	2002	2003
Inflation	2.6%	3.2%	3.4%	3.6%	3.0%
Increases	3.9% (< EUR 733)	4.0%	5.5% (< EUR 352)	3.5% (< EUR 400)	4.0% (< EUR 500)
	3.4% (> EUR 733)		2.75% (< EUR 587)	1.5% (< EUR 620)	2.0% (< EUR 1 000)
			1.4% (< EUR 880)	0.75% (< EUR 910)	0% (> EUR 1 000)
			0% (> EUR 880)	0% (> EUR 910)	

All pensions have 14 monthly payments.

Earnings-related scheme: supplementary component

The full supplementary pension is 20% of the earnings measure under the main component of the earnings-related scheme for workers with 35 years of contributions. The pension is proportionally reduced for shorter contribution periods, implying a linear accrual rate of 0.57%. The value is increased by $1/_{35}$th for each year of contributions (300 days) beyond 35 years.

Minimum pension

The minimum pension is set as 70% of the minimum wage for a married, full-time employee. For 2002, the value was EUR 384 per month, equivalent to around 40% of average earnings. This value is adjusted annually as part of the incomes policy.

Income-tested scheme: social solidarity benefit

This scheme, introduced in 1996, is a non-contributory, means-tested benefit payable from age 60 to low-income pensioners eligible under most schemes (apart from the farmers' pension programme).

Eligibility for benefits under this scheme, known as EKAS, requires that total net income from all sources is less than EUR 6 341 (2003). Total taxable income must not exceed EUR 7 398 and the total taxable family income, EUR 11 312.

Income level, lower limit	0	EUR 5 775	EUR 6 001	EUR 6 152	EUR 6 341
Benefit per month	EUR 111.18	EUR 83.39	EUR 55.59	EUR 27.80	0

Income-tested scheme: uninsured individuals

People who are not entitled to a pension from the social security organisations receive a non-contributory benefit of EUR 170.80 per month from age 65.

Pension modelling results: Greece

Men	Individual earnings, multiple of average					
Women (where different)	0.5	0.75	1	1.5	2	2.5
Gross pension level	42.0	63.0	84.0	126.0	168.0	210.0
(% of average earnings)						
Net pension level	50.3	75.4	99.9	140.8	176.0	210.3
(% of average net earnings)						
Gross replacement rate	84.0	84.0	84.0	84.0	84.0	84.0
(% of individual earnings)						
Net replacement rate	99.9	99.9	99.9	99.9	99.9	99.9
(% of individual net earnings)						
Gross pension wealth	6.3	9.4	12.6	18.9	25.2	31.5
(multiple of average earnings)	*7.3*	*10.9*	*14.5*	*21.8*	*29.1*	*36.3*
Net pension wealth	7.5	11.3	15.0	21.1	26.4	31.5
(multiple of average net earnings)	*8.7*	*13.0*	*17.3*	*24.4*	*30.4*	*36.4*

PENSIONS AT A GLANCE – ISBN 92-64-01871-9 – © OECD 2005

Hungary

The new system combines an earnings-related public pension with mandatory, funded, defined-contribution schemes. This applies to new labour-market entrants and people aged 42 or under at the time of reform. Older workers could choose between this mixed system or a pure pay-as-you-go, public pension. The modelling assumes that workers are covered by the mixed system.

Qualifying conditions

A phased increase in the pension eligibility age will equalise this at 62 for both men and women (from 60 and 55 respectively). The age for men reached 62 in 2000 and will reach 62 for women from the end of 2008. In addition, 20 years' service is required for both the earnings-related pension and the minimum pension. For those retiring before the start of 2009, 15 years' service is required to receive a partial pension.

The reformed system was introduced in June 1998. People who switched voluntarily to the new, mixed system were allowed to return to the pure pay-as-you-go system until the end of 2002. Moreover, the obligation for new entrants to join a private pension fund was suspended in calendar year 2002.

Benefit calculation

Earnings-related

For those covered by the mixed system, the accrual rate is 1.22% of earnings for each year of service (subject to the contribution ceiling, see below). This compares with an accrual rate of 1.65% for those covered by the pay-as-you-go system alone.

The earnings base is currently pay in all years since 1988, moving towards the full lifetime. Earlier years' earnings excluding the last two years' earning before retirement are valorised with economy-wide average earnings.

A ceiling to pensionable earnings was introduced in 1992. In 2002, the ceiling was HUF 2 368 850 (225% of average earnings). There have been increases in the ceiling since 2002. It reached around 2.5 times average earnings in 2003 and 3 times average earnings in 2004. (Note that the modelling uses the 2002 value of the ceiling, indexed to earnings, and does not take account of this increase.)

The pension in payment has been indexed half to wages and half to prices since 2000.

Pension modelling results: Hungary

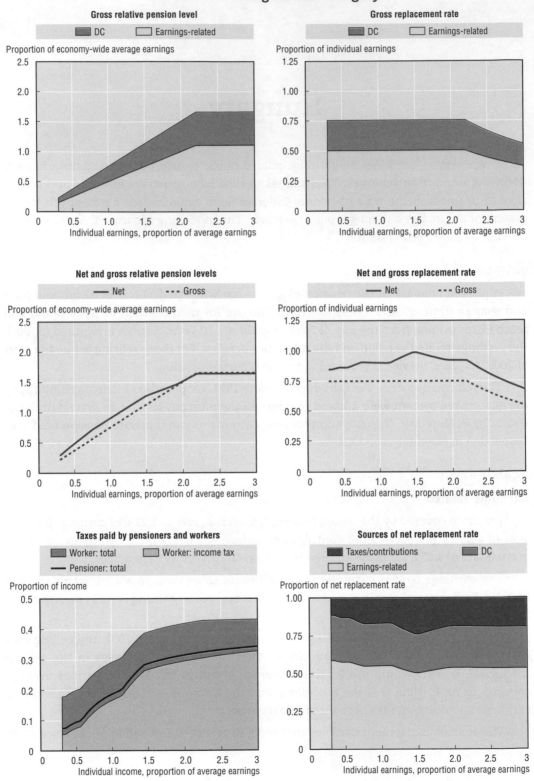

Source: OECD, based on information provided by the countries.

Minimum

There is a minimum pension, which was worth HUF 20 100 per month in 2002 (around 23% of average earnings). The value is indexed in the same way as the earnings-related scheme, that is, half prices and half average earnings. The minimum pension will be abolished from 2009.

Defined contribution

Some 8% of gross pensionable earnings is diverted to the funded plan from 2004 for people covered by the mixed public-private pension option (either by choice or by mandate). This represents an increase from 6% in 2002 and 7% in 2003. The accumulated capital must be converted into an annuity on retirement. The annuity must provide the same mixed indexation of the pension in payment as the public pension scheme. Unisex life tables must be used to calculate annuity rates.

Personal income tax and social security contributions

Taxation of pensioners

There is no additional relief for pensioners beyond the standard tax credit that also applies to people of working age. The earnings-related pension has not been taxable since 2002 while previously it was taxed at a rate of zero. The social security pension is "taxed" when it is awarded. The modelling works on the assumption that the normal tax rules are applied at the point of award.

Taxation of pension income and private pensions

Individual contributions to both the private pension and the public scheme used to attract a credit: 25% of contributions can be deducted from the income-tax liability. This credit was abolished in 2004 (and it has not therefore been modelled). Neither investment returns nor private pension payments are currently taxed.

Social security contributions paid by pensioners

Social security contributions are not levied on pension income.

Pension modelling results: Hungary

Men	Individual earnings, multiple of average					
Women (where different)	0.5	0.75	1	1.5	2	2.5
Gross pension level	37.7	56.5	75.4	113.0	150.7	165.6
(% of average earnings)						
Net pension level	48.9	71.8	90.5	127.7	151.7	164.3
(% of average net earnings)						
Gross replacement rate	75.4	75.4	75.4	75.4	75.4	66.3
(% of individual earnings)						
Net replacement rate	86.6	90.9	90.5	99.1	92.6	81.8
(% of individual net earnings)						
Gross pension wealth	6.1	9.1	12.2	18.3	24.4	26.8
(multiple of average earnings)	7.5	11.3	15.1	22.6	30.1	33.1
Net pension wealth	7.9	11.6	14.6	20.6	24.5	26.6
(multiple of average net earnings)	9.8	14.3	18.1	25.5	30.3	32.8

Iceland

The public pension has three components, including a basic and two income-tested schemes. There are also mandatory occupational pensions with a hybrid (albeit mainly defined-benefit) formula.

Qualifying conditions

The normal pension age is 67. A full basic pension is earned with 40 years' residency. The pension is proportionally reduced for shorter periods of residency, with a minimum of three years required. The pension age is also 67 for members of private-sector occupational plans but is 65 for public-sector workers.

Benefit calculation

Targeted

The full basic pension value is ISK 19 900 per month, equivalent to around 9% of average earnings. This benefit is income-tested: withdrawal begins once income (from sources other than the supplementary pension) exceeds ISK 1 296 060, equivalent to half of average earnings. The withdrawal rate is 30%. This income test applies only to non-pension income, such as earnings or capital income.

A second element is the pension supplement. The maximum value of this benefit is ISK 34 372 per month for a single person, some 16% of average earnings. This benefit is withdrawn against income above ISK 415 894 per year (around 16% of average earnings). The basic pension, however, does not affect the value of the pension supplement. The withdrawal rate for the income test in the pension supplement is 45%.

Finally, there is an additional pension supplement with a maximum entitlement of ISK 15 257 per month, just 7% of average earnings. This is withdrawn against all other income at a rate of two-thirds.

The benefit levels are adjusted in line with public-sector pay (which is assumed here to be equal to the standard assumption of economy-wide earnings growth).

Mandatory occupational

Employer schemes are mandatory. The law requires schemes to target a replacement rate of 56% with 40 years' contributions, giving an accrual rate of 1.4% for each year of service. Coverage is mandatory for people aged 16 to 70. The earnings base in this calculation is average lifetime salary for each year of membership. There is no ceiling to pensionable earnings. Past earnings are effectively valorised in line with prices.

Occupational pensions in payment must by law be increased at least in line with consumer price inflation.

Pension modelling results: Iceland

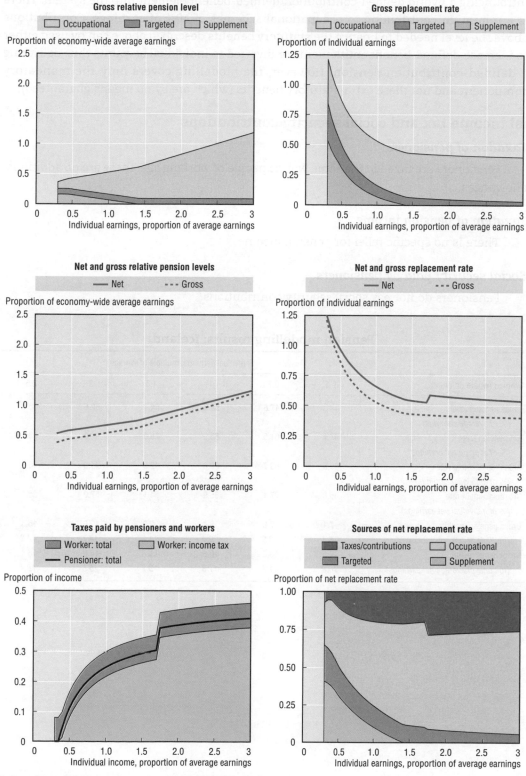

In practice, many schemes pay more than the legal minimum outlined above, typically introducing a hybrid defined-contribution/defined-benefit element into the system. There is a minimum contribution to occupational schemes of 10% of earnings. Contributions above the level needed to finance the statutory benefits described above can by used either to increase defined-benefit entitlements or diverted to individual accounts thus delivering a defined-contribution pension. However, the modelling covers only the mandatory component and not these extra-statutory benefits (which are by no means guaranteed).

Personal income tax and social security contributions

Taxation of pensioners

Pensioners are taxed in the same way as people of working age: there are no additional allowances.

Taxation of pension income

There is no specific relief for pension income.

Social security paid by pensioners

Pensioners do not pay social security contributions.

Pension modelling results: Iceland

Men	Individual earnings, multiple of average					
Women (where different)	0.5	0.75	1	1.5	2	2.5
Gross pension level	42.8	47.8	52.8	64.3	82.6	100.9
(% of average earnings)						
Net pension level	57.1	61.5	65.9	76.0	92.0	108.1
(% of average net earnings)						
Gross replacement rate	85.5	63.7	52.8	42.8	41.3	40.3
(% of individual earnings)						
Net replacement rate	95.8	77.1	65.9	54.1	57.2	55.1
(% of individual net earnings)						
Gross pension wealth	7.1	7.8	8.4	9.9	12.6	15.3
(multiple of average earnings)	*8.1*	*8.8*	*9.4*	*11.1*	*14.1*	*17.2*
Net pension wealth	9.5	10.0	10.5	11.7	14.0	16.4
(multiple of average net earnings)	*10.8*	*11.3*	*11.8*	*13.1*	*15.8*	*18.4*

PENSIONS AT A GLANCE – ISBN 92-64-01871-9 – © OECD 2005

Ireland

The public pension is a basic scheme paying a flat rate to all who meet the contribution conditions. There is also a means-tested pension to provide a safety net for the low-income elderly. Voluntary occupational pension schemes have broad coverage: around half of employees. (The government has a target to increase this proportion to 70%.)

Qualifying conditions

The old-age contributory pension is payable from age 66 while the retirement pension is paid from 65. Full entitlement to both benefits requires an average of 48 weeks contributions or credits per year throughout the working life. The pension value is proportionally reduced for incomplete contribution histories. However, the old-age contributory pension requires a minimum average of 10 weeks' contributions per year and the retirement pension, 24 weeks per year. There is also a minimum total period of contributions of 260 weeks (equivalent to five years' full coverage).

The means-tested pension is payable from age 66.

Benefit calculation

Basic

The values of the old-age contributory pension and the retirement pension are both EUR 147.30 per week (paid for 53 weeks per year), which is around 30% of average earnings. There is an addition of EUR 98.10 for a dependant adult of working age and EUR 113.80 for a dependant age 66 or over. The value of the basic pension under a recent long-term plan is fixed relative to earnings: the target rate is 34% of average earnings.

Pensioners are entitled to many benefits-in-kind. The government estimates that the price of these goods and services would be EUR 724 per year, excluding health benefits. (Note that the modelling covers only cash benefits and not benefits-in-kind.)

Targeted

The maximum value of the means-tested benefit is EUR 134 per week for a single person with an extra EUR 88.50 for an adult dependant. The single person's benefit is worth 28% of average earnings. There is a small disregard in the means test: otherwise, the benefit is withdrawn at 100% of income. There is also an assets test, with capital of more than EUR 20 315 being converted to income using a standard formula.

The value of the target safety-net income in the means-tested scheme broadly follows the uprating of the basic schemes (i.e., linked to earnings).

Pension modelling results: Ireland

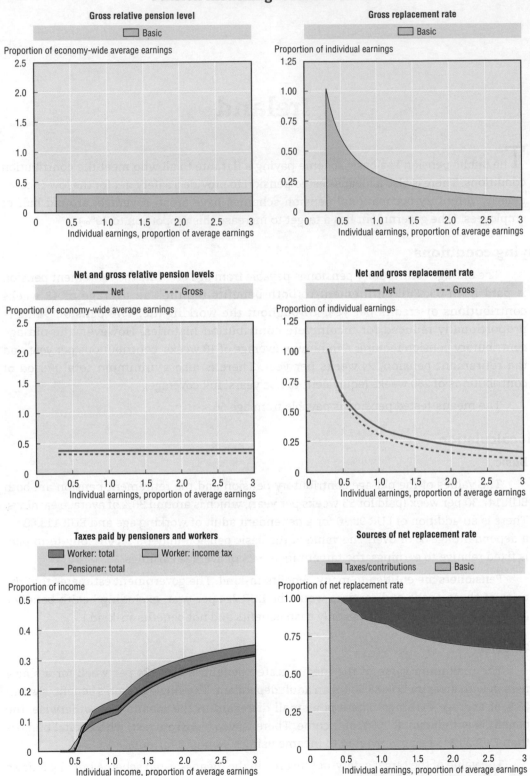

Source: OECD, based on information provided by the countries.

PENSIONS AT A GLANCE – ISBN 92-64-01871-9 – © OECD 2005

Personal income tax and social security contributions

Taxation of pensioners

There is an additional tax credit for over 65s of EUR 205 for single people. This is on top of the general credit, which was EUR 1 520 per person in 2002.

Over 65s are also entitled to a much higher exemption limit (below which no tax is paid). For single people, over 65s have an exemption of EUR 13 000 compared with the general exemption of EUR 5 210.

Taxation of pension income

There are no special rules regarding the taxation of pension income.

Social security contributions paid by pensioners

Pensioners are not liable for social-security contributions.

Pension modelling results: Ireland

Men Women (where different)	Individual earnings, multiple of average					
	0.5	0.75	1	1.5	2	2.5
Gross pension level	30.6	30.6	30.6	30.6	30.6	30.6
(% of average earnings)						
Net pension level	36.6	36.6	36.6	36.6	36.6	36.6
(% of average net earnings)						
Gross replacement rate	61.3	40.9	30.6	20.4	15.3	12.3
(% of individual earnings)						
Net replacement rate	63.0	47.0	36.6	27.4	21.9	18.3
(% of individual net earnings)						
Gross pension wealth	5.4	5.4	5.4	5.4	5.4	5.4
(multiple of average earnings)	6.5	6.5	6.5	6.5	6.5	6.5
Net pension wealth	6.5	6.5	6.5	6.5	6.5	6.5
(multiple of average net earnings)	7.7	7.7	7.7	7.7	7.7	7.7

Italy

The new Italian pension system is based on notional accounts. This is a variant of a traditional pay-as-you-go, public pension system. Contributions earn a rate of return related to GDP growth. Benefits are a function of accumulated notional capital and an actuarial factor (which takes account of average life expectancy at retirement). It applies in full to labour-market entrants from 1996 onwards.

Qualifying conditions

The normal pension age under the new system will be 65 but it will be possible to draw the pension from age 57, subject to five years' contributions being paid. However, the pension value must also be worth at least 1.2 times the social assistance pension. The modelling assumes that people retire at 65.

Benefit calculation

Earnings-related

Under this scheme, the notional accounts of employees are credited with 33% of earnings, which is slightly above the actual contribution rates paid by employees and employers. Contributions are then uprated in line with a five-year moving average of GDP growth until the year of retirement, a process akin to valorisation in a traditional defined-benefit scheme. The baseline assumption in modelling other countries is 2% real wage growth. Given the projected decline in the Italian labour force, a consistent assumption is that real GDP growth is 1.6% per year.

The resulting sum of annual contributions, or "notional capital", is multiplied by a "transformation coefficient" at retirement. This is the corollary of the annuity rate in a funded defined-contribution scheme. (It is the inverse of the "g-value" used in the other OECD countries with notional accounts: Poland and Sweden.) The transformation coefficient varies with the age at which the pension is claimed. The values are reviewed every ten years based on evidence of mortality rates at different ages. Social partners and parliament are consulted but final responsibility rests with government. Actuarial illustrations provided by the Italian government for 2040 (the year used for the baseline projections) are 4.2% at age 57, 4.6% at 60 and 5.3% at age 65. These assume a real interest rate of 1.5%. For modelling purposes, the transformation coefficient is calculated directly from the U.N./World Bank mortality tables for 2040: the coefficient used is 5.7% at age 65.

Minimum pay for contribution purposes is EUR 152 per week (37% of average earnings). Maximum earnings for benefits are EUR 76 443 per year under the new scheme, or nearly 360% of average earnings.

Pension modelling results: Italy

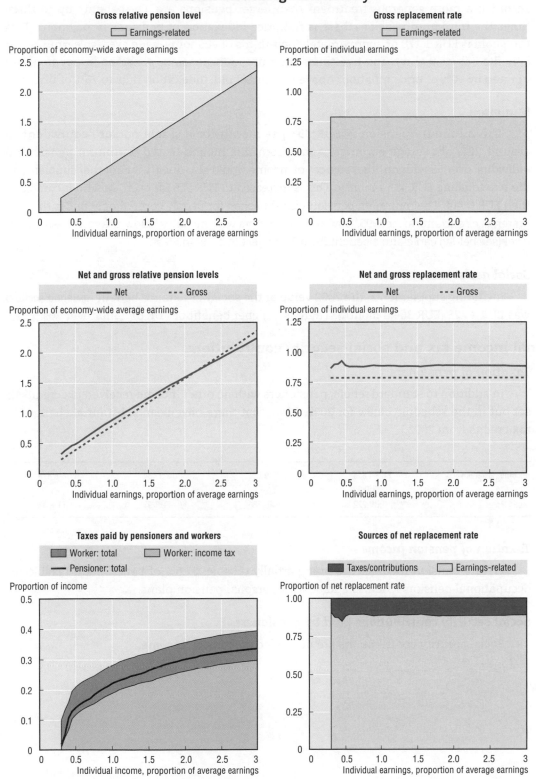

Source: OECD, based on information provided by the countries.

The indexation of pensions in payment is complex, since smaller pensions are accorded a more generous treatment than larger pensions are. For benefits up to three times the minimum pension, there is full price indexation of pensions in payment. This threshold is EUR 1 178 or approximately two-thirds of economy-wide average earnings. For benefits between three and five times the minimum pension, pensions in payment are uprated by 90% of price inflation. Above this threshold, indexation falls to 75% of prices.

Minimum

The minimum pension is EUR 393 per month for a single person, equivalent to around 22% of average earnings. Apart from this means-tested minimum pension an individual over 65 with no other sources of income would also qualify for another supplement, the two totalling EUR 487 a month. This is increased to EUR 516 for over 70s with income less than EUR 6 714. The minimum pension was abolished for people covered only under the new system; i.e., entrants after 1996. However, pensioners with incomes below the social-assistance level (see below) can claim a benefit from 65 subject to a means test.

Social assistance

Including supplements, the 2002 value of the social-assistance benefit (*assegno sociale*) was EUR 4 725 (EUR 364 a month). There is a higher benefit of EUR 6 714 for over 70s.

Personal income tax and social security contributions

Taxation of pensioners

In addition to standard reliefs, pensioners with no other income received tax credits as set out in the schedule below for 2002. (Note that there have been substantial changes to tax credits from 2003.)

Income (lower limit)	EUR 4 855	EUR 9 296	EUR 9 554	EUR 9 813
Age < 75	EUR 98	EUR 62		
Age > 75	EUR 222	EUR 186	EUR 93	EUR 46

Taxation of pension income

Private pension incomes are only partially taxable: 87.5% of benefits are taxable for occupational pension schemes and 60% for personal pension plans.

Social security contributions paid by pensioners

Social security contributions are not levied on pension income.

PENSIONS AT A GLANCE – ISBN 92-64-01871-9 – © OECD 2005

Pension modelling results: Italy

Men	Individual earnings, multiple of average					
Women (where different)	0.5	0.75	1	1.5	2	2.5
Gross pension level	39.4	59.1	78.8	118.2	157.6	197.0
(% of average earnings)						
Net pension level	49.1	69.3	88.8	125.2	159.7	192.0
(% of average net earnings)						
Gross replacement rate	78.8	78.8	78.8	78.8	78.8	78.8
(% of individual earnings)						
Net replacement rate	89.3	88.0	88.8	88.4	89.1	89.0
(% of individual net earnings)						
Gross pension wealth	5.8	8.7	11.4	16.5	22.0	27.5
(multiple of average earnings)	6.9	10.4	13.5	19.4	25.9	32.4
Net pension wealth	7.2	10.2	12.8	17.5	22.3	26.8
(multiple of average net earnings)	8.6	12.2	15.2	20.6	26.3	31.6

Japan

The Japanese public pension system has two tiers: a basic, flat-rate scheme and an earnings-related plan.

Qualifying conditions

The old-age, basic pension is paid from age 65 with a minimum of 25 years' contributions. However, reduced benefits can be received from age 60. The earnings-related pension is paid in addition to the basic pension, with a minimum of one month contribution, provided a pensioner is entitled to the basic pension. The pension age under this programme is gradually being increased from 60 years to reach 65 years for men in 2025 and for women in 2030.

Benefit calculation

Basic

The full basic pension for 2002 was JPY 804 200 per year, corresponding to 19% of average earnings. Average receipt of the basic pension is around JPY 620 000 per year. The value of the basic pension is price indexed.

Earnings-related

The employees' pension scheme has a flat-rate and an earnings-related component. The most important part is the earnings-related pension. The accrual rate was 0.75% of lifetime average earnings, gradually falling to 0.7125%. Past earnings are valorised in line with earnings. There is a ceiling on earnings applied to calculate contributions; it is set at JPY 620 000 a month equivalent to 175% of average earnings.

The flat-rate benefit amounts to JPY 1 676 per month of contributions. This is paid only to pensioners between 60 and 64 years. As the model assumes retirement at 65, this component is not included.

The employees' pension in payment is price indexed.

Personal income tax and social security contributions

Taxation of pensioners

There is an additional JPY 500 000 deduction for over 65s if their income is less than JPY 10 million in total.

There is a schedule of deductions for over 65s, beginning with 100% of the first JPY 1 million of income from the public pension scheme (or from a particular type of private pension scheme: a tax-qualified retirement plan). Next, 25% of income up to JPY 3.6 million is deductible, followed by 15% of income up to JPY 7.2 million and 5%

Pension modelling results: Japan

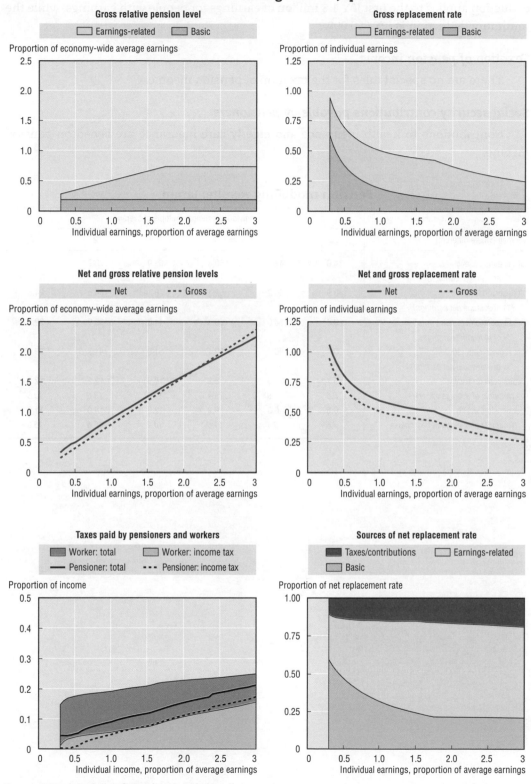

Source: OECD, based on information provided by the countries.

thereafter. Finally, the deduction is subject to a minimum of JPY 1.4 million. The 40% deduction applies to the first JPY 1.8 million of earnings for people with earnings, while the minimum deduction is JPY 650 000.

Taxation of pension income

There are no special rules for the taxation of pension income.

Social security contributions payable by pensioners

Contributions to health insurance and elderly care insurance are levied on pension income.

Pension modelling results: Japan

Men	Individual earnings, multiple of average					
Women (where different)	0.5	0.75	1	1.5	2	2.5
Gross pension level	34.6	42.4	50.3	65.9	73.7	73.7
(% of average earnings)						
Net pension level	40.9	50.2	59.1	76.1	84.5	84.5
(% of average net earnings)						
Gross replacement rate	69.2	56.6	50.3	44.0	36.9	29.5
(% of individual earnings)						
Net replacement rate	80.1	66.3	59.1	51.9	44.3	35.8
(% of individual net earnings)						
Gross pension wealth	5.7	7.0	8.3	10.9	12.2	12.2
(multiple of average earnings)	*6.5*	*7.9*	*9.4*	*12.3*	*13.8*	*13.8*
Net pension wealth	6.8	8.3	9.8	12.6	14.0	14.0
(multiple of average net earnings)	*7.6*	*9.4*	*11.0*	*14.2*	*15.8*	*15.8*

Korea

The Korean public pension scheme was introduced relatively recently. It is an earnings-related scheme with a progressive formula, since benefits are based on both individual earnings and the economy-wide average of earnings.

Qualifying conditions

The pension is available from age 60 provided the individual has contributed for ten years or more. An actuarially reduced early pension can be drawn from age 55.

Benefit calculation

Earnings-related

The scheme is earnings-related. Benefits accrue at the rate of 1.5% of earnings per year of membership up to a maximum replacement rate of 100%. Earlier years' earnings are valorised in line with prices. The earnings measure used in the formula is the average of individual lifetime average earnings and economy-wide average pay (measured over the previous three years). The component of pension based on individual earnings and the part based on average earnings are shown separately in the charts. There is a ceiling to pensionable pay of KRW 3.6 million per month, which is equivalent to double average earnings.

The benefit is indexed to prices after retirement.

Personal income tax and social security contributions

Taxation of pensioners

Pensioners receive an additional allowance of KRW 0.5 million on top of the standard allowance of KRW 1 million.

Taxation of pension income

Pension income is taxable. There is a pension income deduction the thresholds of which are half of those that apply to workers. Below KRW 2.5 million, all income is deductible. Above that level, the marginal rate of deduction falls to 40%, 20% and, finally, to 10%.

Lower limit (KRW)	0	2.5 millions	5 millions	9 millions
Deduction (KRW)	Total amount	2.5 millions	3.5 millions	4.3 millions
Marginal deduction	100%	40%	20%	10%

Social security contributions paid by pensioners

Pensioners do not pay social security contributions.

Pension modelling results: Korea

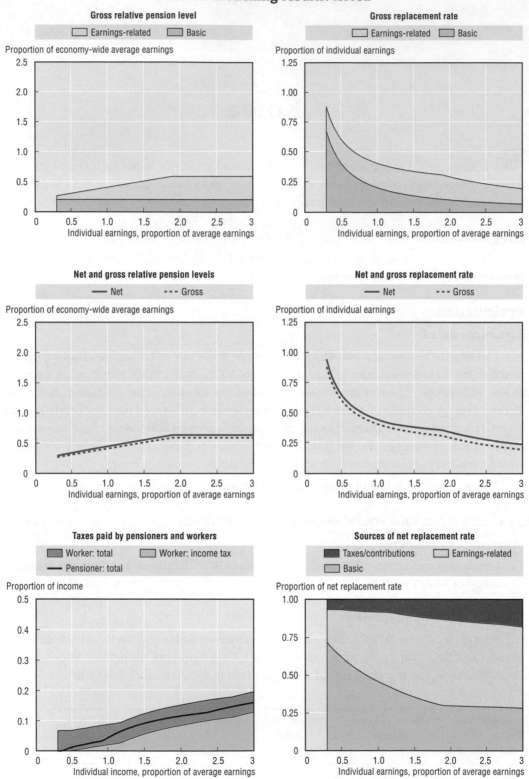

Source: OECD, based on information provided by the countries.

Pension modelling results: Korea

Men	Individual earnings, multiple of average					
Women (where different)	0.5	0.75	1	1.5	2	2.5
Gross pension level	30.5	35.5	40.6	50.8	58.6	58.6
(% of average earnings)						
Net pension level	33.4	38.9	44.3	54.9	63.1	63.1
(% of average net earnings)						
Gross replacement rate	60.9	47.4	40.6	33.8	29.3	23.5
(% of individual earnings)						
Net replacement rate	65.3	51.4	44.3	38.1	34.0	27.8
(% of individual net earnings)						
Gross pension wealth	5.0	5.9	6.7	8.4	9.7	9.7
(multiple of average earnings)	*5.9*	*6.9*	*7.9*	*9.8*	*11.4*	*11.4*
Net pension wealth	5.5	6.4	7.3	9.0	10.4	10.4
(multiple of average net earnings)	*6.5*	*7.5*	*8.6*	*10.6*	*12.2*	*12.2*

Luxembourg

The public pension scheme has two components: a flat-rate part depending on years of coverage and an earnings-related part. There is also a minimum pension.

Qualifying conditions

An early pension is payable from age 57 with 40 years' (compulsory or voluntary) contributions. With 40 years' coverage of compulsory, voluntary or credited contributions, the pension can be paid from age 60. Otherwise, the pension age is 65 (subject to at least ten years' contributions).

Benefit calculation

Basic

This was worth EUR 311 per month in 2002 (from March), subject to 40 years' coverage. This is equivalent to around 12% of average earnings. For incomplete insurance periods, the benefit is reduced proportionally. (Formally, the basic pension is 23.5% of a reference amount, which was EUR 1 323 in 2002.)

There is also an "end-of-year allowance", which adds EUR 42 per month to the pension for 40 years' contributions. This is proportionally reduced for insurance periods under 40 years, implying a little over EUR 1 per month for each year covered. The end-of-year allowance is indexed to nominal earnings (see below).

Earnings-related

The accrual rate for the earnings-related pension is 1.85% per year. The earnings measure used in the formula is lifetime average pay revalued in line with nominal earnings.

The accrual rate is higher for older workers and those with longer contribution periods. For each year of work after age 55, the accrual rate is increased by 0.01 percentage points. Furthermore, each year of contributions beyond 38 also attracts an additional accrual of 0.01 percentage points. The maximum accrual rate is 2.05% per year. Under the standard assumption of a full career starting at age 20, the accrual rate is 2.01%.

The maximum pension in 2002 (from March) was EUR 5 513 per month (formally specified as $^{25}/_6$ of the reference amount). This is just above twice average earnings.

Benefits are automatically indexed to changes in the cost of living (if cumulative inflation is at least 2.5%). In addition, adjustments to increases in real wages must be considered every two years. Recent practice has seen increases close to earnings and the modelling assumes that this practice continues.

Pension modelling results: Luxembourg

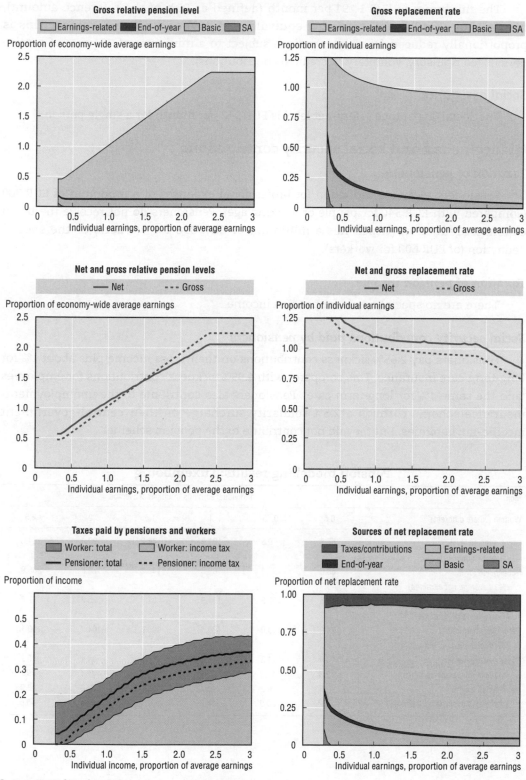

Source: OECD, based on information provided by the countries.

Minimum

The minimum is EUR 1 191 per month (defined as 90% of the reference amount), conditional on 40 years' coverage, equivalent to 46% of average earnings. This is proportionally reduced for shorter periods subject to a minimum of 20 years of service periods (compulsory, voluntary or credited contributions).

Social assistance

The social-assistance safety-net level is EUR 942 per month for a single person.

Personal income tax and social security contributions

Taxation of pensioners

Pensioners receive a deduction for professional expenses of a minimum of EUR 300 (compared with EUR 540 for people of working age). Pensioners do not receive the travel expenses deduction (which has a minimum of EUR 396 for workers) or the special deduction (of EUR 600 for workers).

Taxation of pension income

There are no special reliefs for pension income.

Social security contributions paid by pensioners

Pensioners pay 2.65% sickness contributions on their gross income plus about 1% for long-term care insurance. This compares with 4.95% sickness contributions for employees (and the same 1% for long-term care). Pensioners also contribute to the unemployment-insurance scheme through a 2.5% solidarity surcharge on their central-government income-tax liabilities. But they do not contribute to the pension scheme.

Pension modelling results: Luxembourg

Men	Individual earnings, multiple of average					
Women (where different)	0.5	0.75	1	1.5	2	2.5
Gross pension level	57.7	79.8	101.9	146.2	190.4	224.5
(% of average earnings)						
Net pension level	68.6	90.4	109.8	145.2	178.8	205.9
(% of average net earnings)						
Gross replacement rate	115.5	106.5	101.9	97.4	95.2	89.8
(% of individual earnings)						
Net replacement rate	125.0	115.0	109.8	105.6	104.2	100.1
(% of individual net earnings)						
Gross pension wealth	10.3	14.3	18.3	26.2	34.1	40.2
(multiple of average earnings)	12.8	17.7	22.6	32.3	42.1	49.7
Net pension wealth	12.3	16.2	19.7	26.0	32.0	36.9
(multiple of average net earnings)	15.2	20.0	24.3	32.1	39.6	45.6

Mexico

New labour-force entrants are obliged to join the new funded and privately managed, defined-contribution scheme. The government contributes 5.5% of the 1997 real minimum wage to the individual account. There is also a minimum pension.

Qualifying conditions

Normal retirement age is 65 for men and 60 for women subject to 1 250 weeks (around 25 years) of contribution.

Benefit formula

Funded scheme

Workers and employers contribute a total of 6.275% of earnings to an individual account to which is added a government contribution equivalent to 0.225% of earnings. An additional 5% contribution is made to an individual housing account (a scheme known as *Infonavit*) which reverts to the retirement account when it is not used. Finally, the government contributes 5.5% of the 1997 real minimum wage into all individual retirement accounts.

The calculations assume that the individual converts the accumulated account balance into a price-indexed annuity at normal pension age. Annuity rates are sex-specific.

Minimum pension

The minimum pension is equivalent to the same 1997 real minimum wage value and was estimated to be approximately 23% of the average covered wage in 2002. The link to the real minimum wage means that the minimum pension is effectively price-indexed.

Personal income tax and social security contributions

Taxation of pensioners

The allowance for pensioners is set at 9 times the minimum wage in place of the workers formula based on bonuses and holiday entitlements, *i.e.*, no tax is paid on pensions up to this level.

Taxation of pension income

There are no reliefs for pension income over and above the higher allowance.

Social security contributions paid by pensioners

Pensioners do not pay social security contributions.

Pension modelling results: Mexico

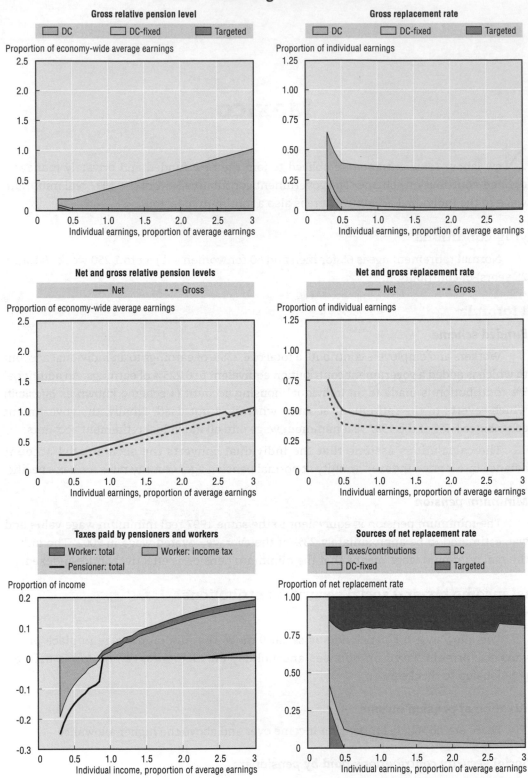

Source: OECD, based on information provided by the countries.

PENSIONS AT A GLANCE – ISBN 92-64-01871-9 – © OECD 2005

Pension modelling results: Mexico

Men	Individual earnings, multiple of average					
Women (where different)	0.5	0.75	1	1.5	2	2.5
Gross pension level	19.6	27.8	36.0	52.4	68.7	85.1
(% of average earnings)	*19.4*	*19.4*	*21.7*	*31.6*	*41.5*	*51.3*
Net pension level	28.1	36.6	45.1	62.1	78.7	95.1
(% of average net earnings)	*27.9*	*27.9*	*30.4*	*40.6*	*50.8*	*61.1*
Gross replacement rate	39.1	37.0	36.0	34.9	34.4	34.1
(% of individual earnings)	*38.8*	*25.9*	*21.7*	*21.1*	*20.7*	*20.5*
Net replacement rate	50.4	46.4	45.1	44.3	44.1	44.2
(% of individual net earnings)	*50.1*	*35.4*	*30.4*	*28.9*	*28.5*	*28.4*
Gross pension wealth	2.6	3.7	4.8	7.0	9.1	11.3
(multiple of average earnings)	*3.6*	*3.6*	*4.1*	*5.9*	*7.8*	*9.6*
Net pension wealth	3.7	4.9	6.0	8.3	10.5	12.6
(multiple of average net earnings)	*5.2*	*5.2*	*5.7*	*7.6*	*9.5*	*11.5*

Netherlands

The Dutch pension system has two main tiers, consisting of a flat-rate public scheme and earnings-related occupational plans. Although there is no statutory obligation for employers to offer a pension scheme to their employees, industrial-relations agreements mean that 91% of employees are covered. These schemes are therefore best thought of as quasi-mandatory.

Qualifying conditions

The basic pension is payable from age 65. Normal retirement age is typically also 65 in occupational plans.

Benefit calculation

Basic

For a single person, the gross pension benefit in 2002 was EUR 11 013, just over a third of average earnings. The benefit value is uprated biannually in line with the net minimum wage.

There is also a social-assistance scheme for older people. Its value is equal to the net basic pension.

Quasi-mandatory occupational

The Netherlands also has a private pension system with broad coverage. The system consists of 64 industry-wide schemes. Under certain conditions, Dutch companies are free to opt out of these plans if they offer their own scheme with equivalent benefits. There are around 866 of these single-employer plans. A further 30 000 (mainly smaller) employers offer schemes operated by insurance companies on their behalf. Of the larger industry and single-employer plans, more than 90% of members are covered by defined-benefit schemes. Of these, around two-thirds use an average salary measure of earnings in the benefit formula, while the rest are based on final salary. Defined-contribution and hybrid schemes make up the remainder of the occupational-pension sector.

There is no statutory requirement for entry ages for occupational plans. In 2003, a little over half of employees were in scheme with no entry age, 6% in schemes with an age of 16-20, 15% with an age of 21-24 and 23% with age 25.

Most final-salary schemes give 1.75% of those earnings for each year of service, implying a replacement rate of 70% after a complete 40-year career. Average-salary plans typically have an accrual rate of 2.25% for each year of service.

There are no legal requirements for valorisation of earlier years' pay and practice varies between schemes according to rules agreed by the social partners. Some schemes valorise with average earnings; others use the same index as used to uprate the value of pensions in payment. Since the latter is also typically average earnings (see below), the modelling assumes an average-salary scheme with valorisation to average earnings.

Pension modelling results: Netherlands

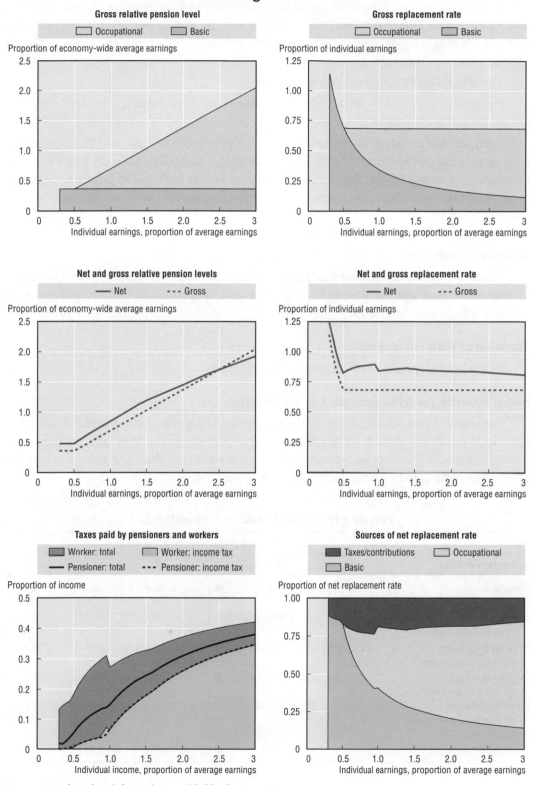

Source: OECD, based on information provided by the countries.

Broad, industry-wide coverage of schemes reduces the problem of lack of portability of occupational pensions. There is a legal requirement to index pension rights of people leaving a scheme before retirement in exactly the same way as pensions in payment are indexed. Vesting periods are very short. Pension rights are fully transferable when people change jobs.

There is no ceiling to pensionable earnings.

Benefits in payment are also typically indexed to earnings (more than half of members are covered in such schemes), although there is no legal uprating requirement.

Occupational pensions are integrated with the public pension system. The current tax rules allow a maximum benefit of 100% of final pay at 65 from both public and private systems. Most schemes have a target total replacement rate of 70% of final pay, so private benefits are reduced by the value of the public pension entitlement, a process known as "franchising".

Personal income tax and social security contributions

Taxation of pensioners

The basic tax credit for over 65s is EUR 737. This tax credit is increased by EUR 289 for incomes less than EUR 28 563. Single people with an income below EUR 28 563 receive an additional tax credit of EUR 256.

Taxation of pension income

There are no special allowances for pension income.

Social security contributions paid by pensioners

Pensioners pay 11.5% of pension income for the general health insurance and survivors' pensions (AWBZ, AWW). Depending on their income, they pay for their own health insurance. The social security contributions are less than the contributions for employees (who also pay for old-age pensions, unemployment, etc.).

Pension modelling results: Netherlands

Men	Individual earnings, multiple of average					
Women (where different)	0.5	0.75	1	1.5	2	2.5
Gross pension level	34.3	51.2	68.3	102.4	136.5	170.6
(% of average earnings)						
Net pension level	46.4	66.3	84.1	118.8	144.7	170.3
(% of average net earnings)						
Gross replacement rate	68.7	68.3	68.3	68.3	68.3	68.3
(% of individual earnings)						
Net replacement rate	82.5	88.2	84.1	85.8	83.8	82.8
(% of individual net earnings)						
Gross pension wealth	5.2	7.7	10.3	15.5	20.6	25.8
(multiple of average earnings)	*5.9*	*8.9*	*11.8*	*17.7*	*23.6*	*29.5*
Net pension wealth	7.0	10.0	12.7	18.0	21.9	25.7
(multiple of average net earnings)	*8.0*	*11.5*	*14.6*	*20.6*	*25.1*	*29.5*

New Zealand

The public pension is flat rate based on a residency test. Occupational schemes are also common.

Qualifying conditions

Ten years' residency since the age of 20 (including five years after age 50) entitles people to the public pension at 65 years of age.

Benefit calculation

Basic

The pension in 2002 for a single person living alone was NZD 288 gross per week, which is around 38% of average earnings. The value is a little lower for people sharing accommodation. It is NZD 437 gross per week for married pensioner couples, equivalent to 58% of average earnings.

The rates of public pension are linked by law to average earnings, with the net couple rate being set between 65% and 72.5% of the net average wage, depending on movements in prices. The rates for single people are set at 65% (living alone) and 60% (sharing) of the couple rate.

Personal income tax and social security contributions

Taxation of pensioners

New Zealand does not provide any tax concessions specifically for older people.

Taxation of pension income

The public pension is subject to personal income tax (in the same manner as any other personal income). Note that the calculations for the worker tax differ slightly from those reported in the OECD's *Taxing Wages*. For workers, these include the 1.2% ACC levy, which is not paid by pensioners. Thus, people of working age pay a very slightly higher average effective tax rate than do pensioners.

Social security contributions paid by pensioners

The New Zealand system is funded through general taxation and not specific social security contributions.

Pension modelling results: New Zealand

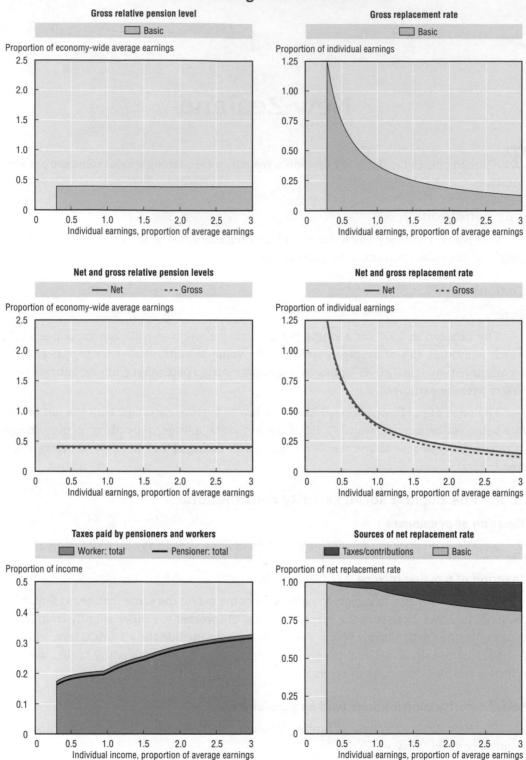

Source: OECD, based on information provided by the countries.

Pension modelling results: New Zealand

Men	Individual earnings, multiple of average					
Women (where different)	0.5	0.75	1	1.5	2	2.5
Gross pension level	37.6	37.6	37.6	37.6	37.6	37.6
(% of average earnings)						
Net pension level	39.5	39.5	39.5	39.5	39.5	39.5
(% of average net earnings)						
Gross replacement rate	75.1	50.1	37.6	25.0	18.8	15.0
(% of individual earnings)						
Net replacement rate	77.1	52.0	39.5	27.9	22.0	18.1
(% of individual net earnings)						
Gross pension wealth	5.7	5.7	5.7	5.7	5.7	5.7
(multiple of average earnings)	*6.5*	*6.5*	*6.5*	*6.5*	*6.5*	*6.5*
Net pension wealth	6.0	6.0	6.0	6.0	6.0	6.0
(multiple of average net earnings)	*6.9*	*6.9*	*6.9*	*6.9*	*6.9*	*6.9*

Norway

The public pension system in Norway consists of a flat-rate, basic pension and a supplementary, earnings-related pension. The benefits of people with little or no small earnings-related pension are topped up with an income-tested supplement.

Qualifying conditions

The normal pension age is 67. Forty years' insurance is required to receive the full pension, both basic and earnings-related benefits. Both benefits are proportionally reduced for shorter insurance histories. A minimum of three years of contributions is required to receive an earnings-related pension.

Benefit calculation

Basic

Many benefits under the National Insurance Scheme are determined in relation to a basic amount, G, that was NOK 53 233 (on average) in 2002. The full basic pension for a single pensioner equals the basic amount, which is equivalent to 18% of average earnings. There is no formal indexation procedure for the value of the basic amount/pension. Although past increases were below earnings growth, in recent years the government has agreed to increase the basic pension in line with average earnings. The modelling assumes that this practice continues.

Earnings-related

Since the basic pension replaces the first slice of earnings, the earnings-related scheme only covers earnings above the value of the basic amount. The earnings-related scheme has a progressive formula, i.e., the replacement rate falls for higher earnings. Annual earnings between 2.89 times the basic amount and six times the basic amount are replaced at a 42% rate. Between 6 and 12 times the basic amount, the replacement rate is one third of that level (that is, 14%). Given that 40 years' contributions are needed for a full pension, these are equivalent to annual accrual rates of 1.05 and 0.35% respectively. The first threshold, where the accrual rate declines, is a little over average earnings (109%). The ceiling on earnings eligible for benefits is therefore a little over double average earnings (219%).

The calculation of the pension uses the best 20 years of earnings. It is specified as a points system. Thus, the valorisation of earlier years' accruals depends on the adjustment procedure for the value of the basic amount. As discussed previously, the modelling assumes that the basic amount will in future be uprated in line with average earnings.

Pension modelling results: Norway

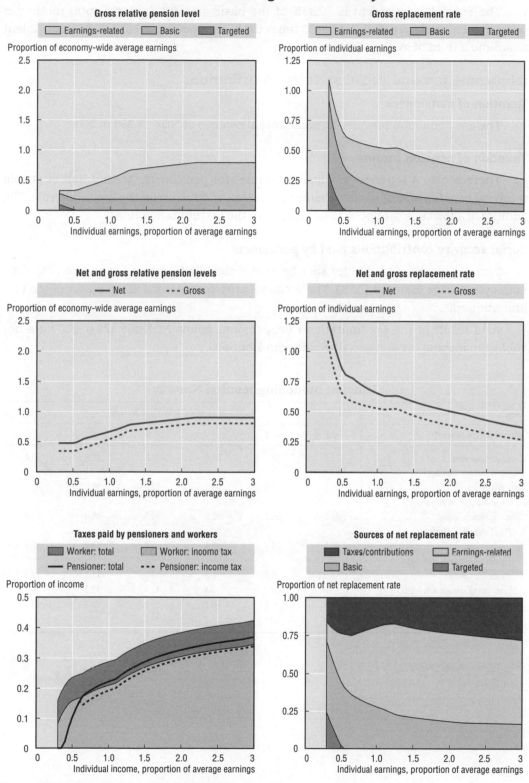

Source: OECD, based on information provided by the countries.

Targeted supplement

The special supplement is 79.33% of the basic amount, giving a total minimum pension for a single pensioner of 1.7933 times the basic amount, *i.e.* NOK 95 463, equivalent to around a third of average earnings.

Personal income tax and social security contributions

Taxation of pensioners

The age deduction provides an additional allowance of NOK 18 360 in 2002.

Taxation of pension income

There is also a separate "tax-limitation rule" for pensioners. Around half of people receiving benefits and/or pensions either pay no tax or do so under the limitation rule. The additional allowance cannot be used along with the tax-limitation rule.

Social security contributions paid by pensioners

Pension income is liable for social security contribution at a lower rate (3%) than employees' wage earnings (7.8%). The social security contribution is not a part of the tax-limitation rule.

As a result of the tax-limitation rule, pensions below NOK 105 325 in 2002 are not subject to income tax and social security contributions.

Pension modelling results: Norway

Men	Individual earnings, multiple of average					
Women (where different)	0.5	0.75	1	1.5	2	2.5
Gross pension level	32.7	42.1	52.6	69.8	76.8	79.4
(% of average earnings)						
Net pension level	45.9	56.6	65.1	80.0	86.8	89.3
(% of average net earnings)						
Gross replacement rate	65.3	56.1	52.6	46.5	38.4	31.8
(% of individual earnings)						
Net replacement rate	85.5	73.1	65.1	58.2	50.1	42.8
(% of individual net earnings)						
Gross pension wealth	5.3	6.7	8.2	10.7	11.7	12.1
(multiple of average earnings)	*6.2*	*7.7*	*9.5*	*12.4*	*13.5*	*14.0*
Net pension wealth	7.4	9.0	10.1	12.2	13.2	13.6
(multiple of average net earnings)	*8.7*	*10.4*	*11.7*	*14.2*	*15.3*	*15.7*

Poland

The new pension system applies to people born in 1949 or after, that is aged 50 at the time of the reform. The new public scheme is based on a system of notional accounts. People under 30 (born in 1969 and after) at the time of the reform must also participate in the funded scheme; people aged 30-50 (born between 1949 and 1968) could choose the funded option. However, the choice had to be made in 1999 and it was irrevocable.

Qualifying conditions

The minimum pension age in the new system will be 65 for men and 60 for women. For the minimum pension, 25 and 20 years' contributions are required from men and women, respectively.

Benefit calculation

Earnings-related

A contribution of 12.22% of earnings will be credited to individuals' notional accounts. These contributions are uprated between the time they are made and the time of retirement by price inflation plus 75% of the growth of the real covered wage bill. From 2004 onwards, the notional interest rate will be defined as 100% of the growth of the real covered wage bill and no less than price inflation.

At retirement, accumulated notional capital is divided by the "g-value" to arrive at the pension benefit. The g-value is average life expectancy at retirement age: this process is equivalent to the process of annuitisation in funded pension systems. The g-value is calculated using the actuarial data from the United Nations/World Bank population database.

There is a ceiling to contributions and pensionable earnings of PLN 64 620. The policy is to set the ceiling at 2½ times projected average earnings for a given year.

Pensions in payment are uprated in line with 80% of prices and 20% of average earnings. Note, however, that the 2004 government proposal includes a shift to prices from 2005.

Minimum pension

The minimum pension was PLN 530 per month in 2001-02 and PLN 533 in 2002-03. The model uses the average value for calendar 2002. The minimum pension target is adjusted to 80% inflation plus 20% of wage growth.

Defined contribution

Some 7.3 percentage points of the total contribution are diverted to the funded scheme for those compulsorily covered or choosing this option. At retirement, the

Pension modelling results: Poland

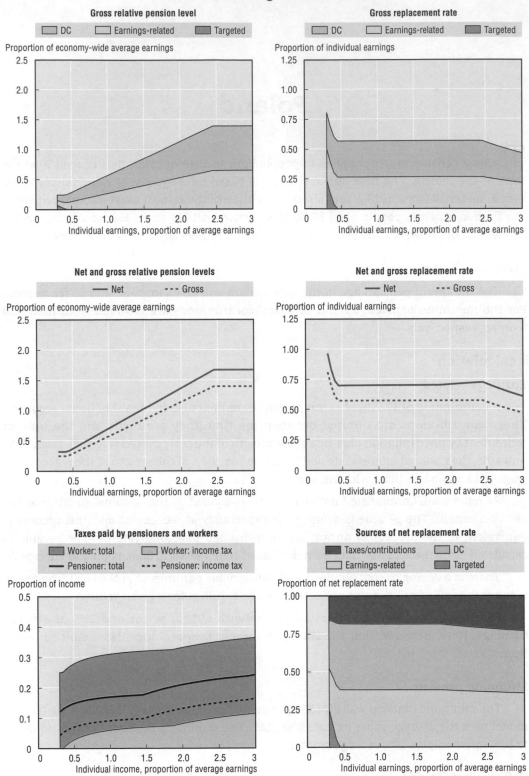

Source: OECD, based on information provided by the countries.

accumulated capital must be converted to an annuity. At the minimum, this must be price-indexed (which is used in the model calculation). Annuity rates will most likely have to be based on unisex life-tables though this has not been decided yet.

Personal and income tax and social security contributions

Taxation of pensioners

There is no specific tax relief for pensioners.

Taxation of pension income

There are no special rules for the taxation of pension income. [Employees can deduct PLN 1 444 for 2002 from their incomes for work-related expenses (although this varies with the number of workplaces and whether the workplace is the same as the dwelling). Of course, this deduction does not apply to pensioners.]

Social security contributions paid by pensioners

Pension income is not subject to contributions for pensions, unemployment insurance etc. However, there is a tax-deductible health-insurance contribution of 7.75%. This contribution started to increase by 0.25 percentage points each year from 2003 to reach the level of 9%, but only 7.75% will be tax deductible. The contribution is paid by both pensioners and workers.

Pension modelling results: Poland

Men	Individual earnings, multiple of average					
Women (where different)	0.5	0.75	1	1.5	2	2.5
Gross pension level	28.4	42.6	56.9	85.3	113.7	139.4
(% of average earnings)	*24.2*	*31.0*	*41.4*	*62.1*	*82.8*	*101.5*
Net pension level	36.4	53.0	69.7	103.1	136.5	166.7
(% of average net earnings)	*31.4*	*39.4*	*51.6*	*75.9*	*100.2*	*122.1*
Gross replacement rate	56.9	56.9	56.9	56.9	56.9	55.8
(% of individual earnings)	*48.4*	*41.4*	*41.4*	*41.4*	*41.4*	*40.6*
Net replacement rate	69.6	69.7	69.7	69.8	70.5	71.0
(% of individual net earnings)	*60.1*	*51.8*	*51.6*	*51.3*	*51.7*	*52.0*
Gross pension wealth	4.0	5.9	7.9	11.9	15.8	19.4
(multiple of average earnings)	*4.8*	*6.1*	*8.2*	*12.3*	*16.4*	*20.1*
Net pension wealth	5.1	7.4	9.7	14.4	19.0	23.2
(multiple of average net earnings)	*6.2*	*7.8*	*10.2*	*15.0*	*19.8*	*24.1*

Portugal

An earnings-related public pension scheme with a means-tested safety net.

Qualifying conditions

The standard pension age is 65 although early retirement is possible from age 55. A minimum of 15 years of contributions are also required for retirement at 65. Early retirement is possible with 30 years of contributions.

Benefit calculation

Earnings-related

The pension accrues at 2% of the earnings base for each year of contributions for 20 or fewer years' contributions. For beneficiaries with 21 or more years of contributions, the accrual rate ranges between 2% and 2.3% depending on earnings. The schedule for the accrual rate depends on individual earnings relative to the value of the national minimum wage.

Earnings/minimum wage	< 1.1	1.1-2.0	2.0-4.0	4.0-8.0	> 8.0
Accrual rate (%)	2.3	2.25	2.2	2.1	2.0

Pension accrues for a maximum of 40 years.

The earnings measure is presently the best 10 of the final 15 years. However, this base is currently being extended, such that it will reach lifetime average earnings from 2017. Valorisation of earnings from the beginning of 2002 is to a mix of earnings and prices. The weights are 75% price inflation and 25% earnings growth, subject to a maximum real increase of 0.5%.

Pensions in payment are indexed to prices.

Minimum

There is a minimum pension of EUR 190 (for workers with up to 15 years of contributions). For workers with 15 to 40 years, the amount of the minimum pension varies between 65% and 100% of the minimum wage net of employee's social contributions. For 2002, this was EUR 201 and EUR 310 respectively.

There are 14 monthly payments.

Pension modelling results: Portugal

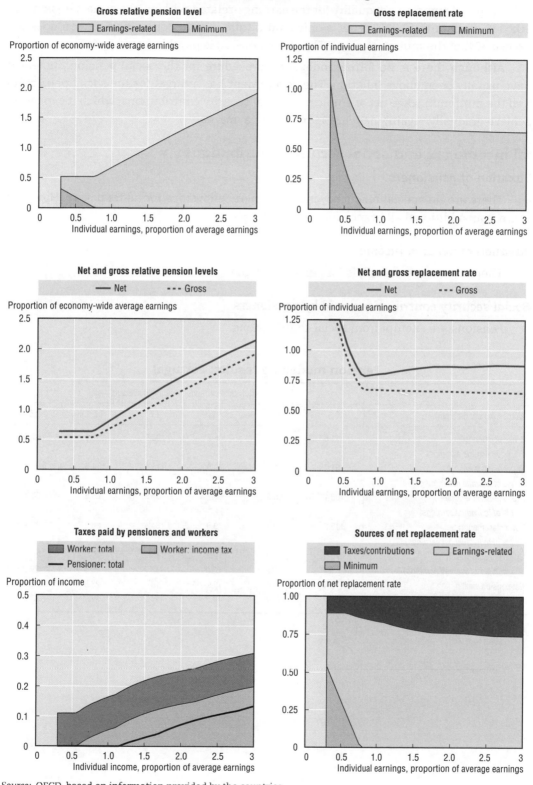

Source: OECD, based on information provided by the countries.

Targeted

For people who do not qualify for the earnings-related scheme, the social pension was EUR 138 per month in 2002. This is only paid if total income for a single person does not exceed 30% of the minimum wage. The social pension is payable from age 65.

Although there is no formal indexation procedure for the social pension, increases have usually been above inflation. The government has a target for the social pension of half the minimum wage net of employee's social security contributions, which it expects to achieve gradually. Again, there are 14 monthly payments.

Personal income tax and social security contributions

Taxation of pensioners

There are no special reliefs beyond the general allowance for all taxpayers. However, there is an additional allowance for disabled people.

Taxation of pension income

There are no special reliefs for pension income.

Social security contributions paid by pensioners

Pensions are exempt from social contributions.

Pension modelling results: Portugal

Men	Individual earnings, multiple of average					
Women (where different)	0.5	0.75	1	1.5	2	2.5
Gross pension level	51.6	51.6	66.7	98.9	131.1	161.8
(% of average earnings)						
Net pension level	61.7	61.7	79.8	118.4	154.5	186.4
(% of average net earnings)						
Gross replacement rate	103.1	68.8	66.7	65.9	65.5	64.7
(% of individual earnings)						
Net replacement rate	115.9	79.8	79.8	84.4	86.3	86.9
(% of individual net earnings)						
Gross pension wealth	7.9	7.9	10.2	15.1	20.0	24.7
(multiple of average earnings)	9.2	9.2	12.0	17.7	23.5	29.0
Net pension wealth	9.4	9.4	12.2	18.1	23.6	28.5
(multiple of average net earnings)	11.1	11.1	14.3	21.2	27.7	33.4

PENSIONS AT A GLANCE – ISBN 92-64-01871-9 – © OECD 2005

Slovak Republic

The earnings-related, public scheme has recently been transformed from a standard defined-benefit formula to a point system. There is a minimum annual pension accrual related to the minimum wage.

Qualifying conditions

The normal pension age is gradually increasing to 62 for men and women, reaching 62 for women in 2014. Eligibility depends on making at least 10 years of contributions.

Benefit calculation

Earnings-related

The new pension formula applies from 2004. Pension points are calculated as the ratio of individual earnings to average earnings. Each pension point is for 2004 worth SKK 183.58. This point value is indexed to average earnings.

Based on Slovak government estimates of 7.8% nominal wage growth in 2004 and actual wage growth of 6.3% in 2003, the pension-point value for 2002 would have been SKK 160.18. (Note that for comparison with other countries, the calculations are based on the parameters had the reformed pension system been in operation in 2002.) Average earnings in 2002 were SKK 13 511 per month. (Note that this national figure differs from average earnings calculated under standard OECD methodology.) Dividing the point value by the national average earnings figure gives the equivalent to the accrual rate in a defined-benefit scheme, which is just under 1.2%.

There was a maximum pension of SKK 8 282 in the first half of 2002 and SKK 8 697 in the second half. However, this is abolished under the new points-based system. Instead, there is a ceiling to pensionable earnings fixed in 2003 at three times average earnings. Based on the 2002 average earnings number, the ceiling would have been SKK 486 396 in that year.

Pensions in payment are indexed to the arithmetic average of earnings growth and price inflation.

Minimum

The minimum pension is abolished under the new system. However, there is a mechanism to lift low pensionable earnings to the level of the minimum wage, which for 2004 is SKK 6 080. In 2002, the minimum wage was SKK 4 920 until October, when it was increased to SKK 5 570.

Pension modelling results: Slovak Republic

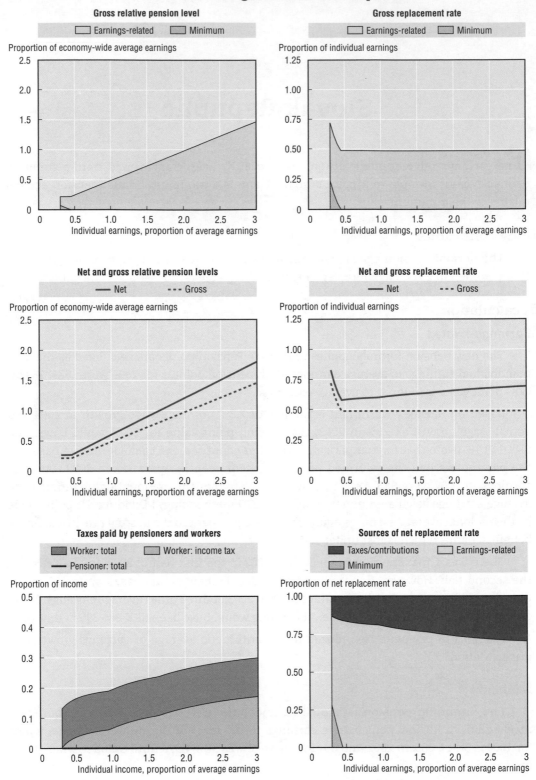

Source: OECD, based on information provided by the countries.

Personal income tax and social security contributions

Taxation of pensioners

There are no special tax allowances or credits for pensioners.

Taxation of pension income

Pensions are not taxed.

Social security contributions paid by pensioners

Pensioners do not pay social security contributions.

Pension modelling results: Slovak Republic

Men Women (where different)	Individual earnings, multiple of average					
	0.5	0.75	1	1.5	2	2.5
Gross pension level *(% of average earnings)*	24.3	36.4	48.6	72.9	97.2	121.5
Net pension level *(% of average net earnings)*	30.1	45.2	60.2	90.4	120.5	150.6
Gross replacement rate *(% of individual earnings)*	48.6	48.6	48.6	48.6	48.6	48.6
Net replacement rate *(% of individual net earnings)*	58.2	59.4	60.2	63.1	65.7	67.8
Gross pension wealth *(multiple of average earnings)*	4.0 *4.9*	6.0 *7.3*	8.0 *9.8*	12.0 *14.6*	15.9 *19.5*	19.9 *24.4*
Net pension wealth *(multiple of average net earnings)*	4.9 *6.0*	7.4 *9.1*	9.9 *12.1*	14.8 *18.1*	19.8 *24.2*	24.7 *30.2*

Spain

The Spanish public pension system consists of a single, earnings-related benefit. There is also a means-tested minimum pension, which replaces the previous special social assistance scheme.

Qualifying conditions

The retirement age for a full benefit is 65 years for men and women. 15 years of contributions are necessary to qualify for a pension benefit.

Benefit calculation

Earnings-related

The benefit accrues according to a schedule. After 15 years' contributions, it is 50% of the earnings base. Over the next 10 years, an extra 3% is accrued per year, followed by 2% per year thereafter. The maximum accrual is 100%, reached after 35 years' contributions.

The earnings base is pay over the last 15 years, up-rated in line with prices, apart from the last two years. This means that the maximum replacement rate relative to final salary is less than 100%. On the standard assumptions for earnings growth and price inflation, this is calculated to be 88%. There is a ceiling to earnings for contributions and benefit purposes of EUR 30 899, or 191% of average earnings.

Benefits are price-indexed.

Minimum

There is a minimum pension payable from age 65 amounting to EUR 393 per month. There are 14 payments per year.

Personal income tax and social security contributions

Taxation of pensioners

There are no special rules for the taxation of pensioners.

Taxation of pension income

There are no special allowances for pension income.

Social security contributions paid by pensioners

Social security contributions are not levied on pension income.

PENSIONS AT A GLANCE – ISBN 92-64-01871-9 – © OECD 2005

Pension modelling results: Spain

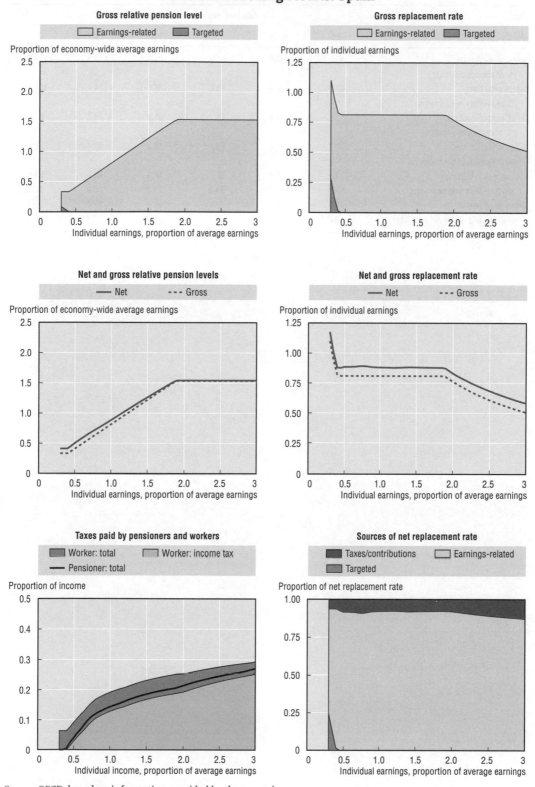

Pension modelling results: Spain

Men	Individual earnings, multiple of average					
Women (where different)	0.5	0.75	1	1.5	2	2.5
Gross pension level	40.6	60.9	81.2	121.8	153.3	153.3
(% of average earnings)						
Net pension level	49.9	69.9	88.3	126.0	154.1	154.1
(% of average net earnings)						
Gross replacement rate	81.2	81.2	81.2	81.2	76.7	61.3
(% of individual earnings)						
Net replacement rate	88.7	89.4	88.3	88.4	83.4	68.8
(% of individual net earnings)						
Gross pension wealth	6.1	9.1	12.2	18.3	23.0	23.0
(multiple of average earnings)	*7.1*	*10.7*	*14.3*	*21.4*	*26.9*	*26.9*
Net pension wealth	7.5	10.5	13.2	18.9	23.1	23.1
(multiple of average net earnings)	*8.8*	*12.3*	*15.5*	*22.1*	*27.1*	*27.1*

Sweden

The new pension system, introduced in 1999, applies to people aged 45 or under at the time of reform. The old and the new systems will cover older workers proportionally: people born 1938-53 will receive pensions under a mix of the old and new rules. The earnings-related part is based on notional accounts. There is a small mandatory contribution to individual, defined-contribution pensions and an income-tested top-up. Occupational pension plans – with defined-benefit and defined-contribution elements – have broad coverage.

Qualifying conditions

Eligibility for the guarantee pension will be earned with three years' residency. Maximum pension is earned with 40 years' residency and is reduced proportionally for shorter periods. The standard pension age for occupational plans is 65 with an early pension age of 55 and there is a minimum entry age of 28. The earnings-related, public pension can be claimed from 61.

Benefit calculation

Earnings-related

The new earnings-related scheme – the "income pension" – uses notional accounts. Contributions of 16% of pensionable pay are credited and then up-rated in line with a three-year moving average of economy-wide earnings. Pensionable pay is defined as earnings less the employee contribution of 7%, giving an effective contribution rate on gross earnings of 14.88%. Contributions are only levied when earnings exceed a small floor of SEK 11 310 in 2002, less than 5% of average earnings, although they are due on the whole of earnings for all people earning above the floor. There is a ceiling to benefits calculated in terms of pensionable earnings of SEK 291 000 in 2002. However, this again relates to pensionable earnings, giving an effective ceiling relative to gross earnings of SEK 313 116 in 2002 (around 130% of average earnings). There is no ceiling on employer contributions even though pension rights do not accrue on earnings above the ceiling.

At retirement, the accumulated notional capital will be converted to an annuity. This calculation will use a coefficient dependent on individual retirement age and contemporaneous life expectancy (based on the previous five years' unisex mortality table). A real return of 1.6% a year will be assumed in this calculation. Illustrative values for the annuity coefficient at age 65 are 15.4 for 2000 rising to 15.9 by 2020. The annuity coefficient is currently 18.2 for retirement at 61 and 13.0 at age 70.

After retirement, pensions are uprated with average earnings less a "growth norm" of 1.6%. Real wage growth short of this norm means that real pensions will fall. There is also a "balance mechanism": if assets (the buffer fund plus the estimated value of assets in

Pension modelling results: Sweden

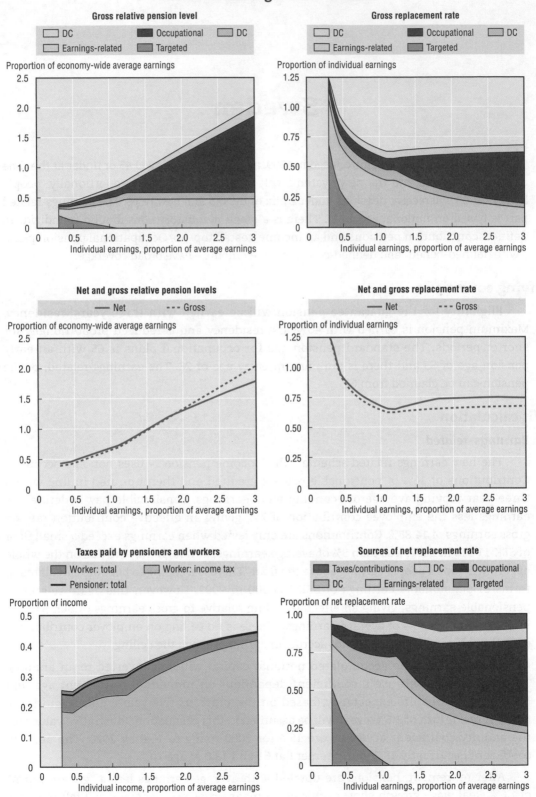

Gross relative pension level

DC   Occupational   DC
Earnings-related   Targeted

Proportion of economy-wide average earnings

Individual earnings, proportion of average earnings

Gross replacement rate

DC   Occupational   DC
Earnings-related   Targeted

Proportion of individual earnings

Individual earnings, proportion of average earnings

Net and gross relative pension levels

— Net   --- Gross

Proportion of economy-wide average earnings

Individual earnings, proportion of average earnings

Net and gross replacement rate

— Net   --- Gross

Proportion of individual earnings

Individual earnings, proportion of average earnings

Taxes paid by pensioners and workers

Worker: total   Worker: income tax
— Pensioner: total

Proportion of income

Individual income, proportion of average earnings

Sources of net replacement rate

Taxes/contributions   DC   Occupational
DC   Earnings-related   Targeted

Proportion of net replacement rate

Individual earnings, proportion of average earnings

Source: OECD, based on information provided by the countries.

the form of contribution revenues) fall below liabilities (pensions) then indexation of pensions in payment and returns credited to notional accounts are reduced in order to restore the balance between liabilities and assets.

For modelling purposes, the annuity coefficients are calculated using the above rules and the relevant mortality data from the United Nations/World Bank population database. It is assumed that the balance mechanism does not affect the uprating of benefits.

Targeted

The "guarantee pension" is an income-tested top-up for people with low levels of benefit from notional accounts. For a single person, the guaranteed benefit in 2002 was SEK 80 727 (formally, equal to the 2002 price base amount) or 33% of average earnings.

The guarantee pension is withdrawn at 100% against the first SEK 47 754 (2002) of income from the earnings-related pension, thereafter at 48%. This threshold is equivalent to 20% of average earnings. Only when earnings-related pension exceeds SEK 116 353 – nearly 50% of average earnings – is entitlement to the guarantee exhausted.

The guarantee level is price indexed.

Defined contribution

A further 2.5% of pensionable income (giving an effective contribution rate against gross earnings of 2.325%) will be paid into personal pension accounts: the premium pension. People have a broad choice of where these funds are invested.

At retirement, a new public agency will be responsible for converting the accumulated balance into an annuity. Alternatively, people will be able to choose a variable annuity, where their funds continue to be invested by their chosen fund manager. These annuities do not have a guaranteed value.

Voluntary occupational

The four major occupational schemes together cover 90% of employees. The modelling uses the ITP scheme for white-collar workers, which mixes defined-benefit and defined-contribution elements.

The defined benefit is 10% of final salary on earnings up to a ceiling specified as 7.5 times the base amount or SEK 291 000 in 2002. However, this threshold is in practice lower than the effective ceiling to the public scheme because it applies to gross earnings rather than pensionable earnings. Between this threshold and around 3.1 times average earnings, the full-career replacement rate is 65%; and from around 3.1 to 4.6 times average earnings, 32.5%. A full pension is earned with 30 years' contributions from an entry age of 28. Shorter tenures result in a proportionally reduced benefit.

Pensions in payment are adjusted at the discretion of the ITP board. However, recent increases have been broadly in line with price inflation and so this procedure is assumed in the modelling.

The ITP also has a defined-contribution component, which receives a contribution of 2% of gross earnings. The modelling assumes that this is withdrawn at the normal pension age in the form of a price-indexed annuity. The entry age is again 28.

Personal income tax and social security contributions

Taxation of pensioners

Older people are entitled to a special income-tax deduction of between SEK 11 104 and SEK 59 688 (depending on pension income). This extra deduction is withdrawn at 66.5% of income above the minimum pension level, implying no special deduction for pensioners with incomes above SEK 132 605.

These concessions were abolished in 2003 as part of the policy package that included the introduction of the guarantee pension. Since the aim of the modelling is to capture the long-term structure and parameters of the pension system, the system modelled includes the guarantee pension but without the additional tax concessions.

Taxation of pension income

There are no special allowances for pension income.

Social security contributions paid by pensioners

Social security contributions are not levied on pension income.

Pension modelling results: Sweden

Men	Individual earnings, multiple of average					
Women (where different)	0.5	0.75	1	1.5	2	2.5
Gross pension level	43.9	54.4	64.8	96.9	132.4	167.8
(% of average earnings)						
Net pension level	48.1	58.4	68.2	98.7	129.9	155.1
(% of average net earnings)						
Gross replacement rate	87.8	72.5	64.8	64.6	66.2	67.1
(% of individual earnings)						
Net replacement rate	90.2	76.4	68.2	70.1	74.3	75.0
(% of individual net earnings)						
Gross pension wealth	7.0	8.7	10.4	15.5	21.0	26.6
(multiple of average earnings)	7.8	9.6	11.4	16.7	23.0	29.3
Net pension wealth	7.7	9.3	10.9	15.8	20.6	24.5
(multiple of average net earnings)	8.6	10.4	12.1	17.0	22.8	27.3

Switzerland

The Swiss pension system has three main parts. The public scheme is earnings-related, but has a progressive formula. There is also a system of mandatory occupational pensions and an income-tested supplementary benefit.

Qualifying conditions

Pensionable age under the public scheme and mandatory occupational pensions is currently 65 for men and 63 for women, although the latter will increase to 64 by 2005.

Benefit calculation

Earnings-related

The public pension is based on average lifetime earnings. If this figure is less than CHF 37 080, then the entitlement is CHF 9 146 plus 26% of average lifetime earnings. For lifetime earnings above the threshold, the entitlement is a flat CHF 12 854 plus 16% of average lifetime earnings.

There is a minimum pension of CHF 12 360 and a maximum pension of twice that level. These are equivalent to 20 and 40% of average earnings, respectively. The maximum benefit is reached when earnings are CHF 74 160, equivalent to 115% of economy-wide average earnings.

Pensions in payment are indexed 50% to prices and 50% to nominal earnings.

Mandatory occupational

The system of mandatory occupational pensions was introduced in 1985. It is built around "defined credits" to an individual's pension account. These vary by sex and age:

Men, of age	25-34	35-44	45-54	55-64
Women, of age	25-31	32-41	42-51	52-63
Credit (% of co-ordinated earnings)	7	10	15	18

The value of accumulated credits at retirement naturally depends on the required interest rate applied to earlier years' contributions. This was, for a long period until the end of 2002, 4% but was cut to 3.25% from 2003 with a further reduction planned. If the interest rate is broadly equivalent to the growth rate of earnings, then a full career in the system will give a man at age 65 accumulated credits of 500% of earnings. However, higher (or lower) outcomes are possible if the interest rate exceeds (is less than) growth in earnings. The modelling assumes that the interest rate applied to the credits will be equivalent to earnings over the long term.

Pension modelling results: Switzerland

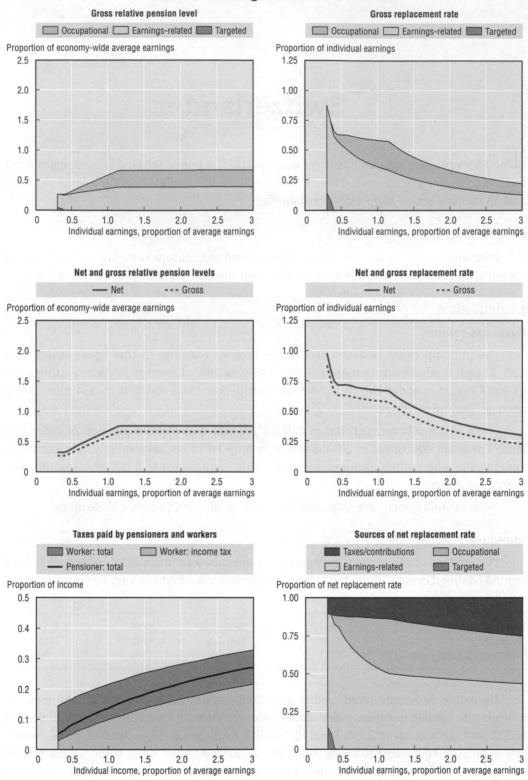

Source: OECD, based on information provided by the countries.

The system has a minimum annuity rate of 7.2% that is applied to this notional capital sum. This gives a full career replacement rate of (500 × 7.2 =) 36% (subject to the interest rate being equal to earnings growth).

The defined credits (and hence the replacement rate) apply only to "co-ordinated" earnings. This is pay between the maximum pension of the public scheme (CHF 24 720) and three times that level (CHF 74 160). These thresholds are equivalent to 38 and 115% of average earnings. Note that the ceiling for pensionable pay is the same in the public scheme and in the mandatory occupational pension sector.

Targeted

The supplementary benefit scheme aims to give a minimum pension income to single people of at least CHF 16 880, equivalent to 26% of average earnings. The supplementary benefit is indexed in the same way as the public old age pensions, i.e. to a mixed index of 50% prices and 50% wages. There are discretionary cantonal additions for low-income pensioners; these are disregarded in the model.

Personal income tax and social security contributions

Taxation of pensioners

Swiss cantons often grant pensioners an additional allowance but there is no extra allowance in the Federal income tax. Note that the modelling assumes a resident of the city of Zurich in the canton of Zurich.

Taxation of pension income

There are no special allowances for pension income.

Social security contributions paid by pensioners

Social security contributions are not levied on pension income.

Pension modelling results: Switzerland

Men	Individual earnings, multiple of average					
Women (where different)	0.5	0.75	1	1.5	2	2.5
Gross pension level	31.4	45.2	58.2	66.3	66.3	66.3
(% of average earnings)	31.5	45.6	58.8	67.1	67.1	67.1
Net pension level	37.8	53.1	67.3	75.7	75.7	75.7
(% of average net earnings)	38.0	53.6	68.0	76.6	76.6	76.6
Gross replacement rate	62.8	60.2	58.2	44.2	33.1	26.5
(% of individual earnings)	63.0	60.7	58.8	44.7	33.5	26.8
Net replacement rate	71.4	68.9	67.3	53.0	41.4	34.3
(% of individual net earnings)	71.6	69.5	68.0	53.6	41.8	34.7
Gross pension wealth	5.5	7.9	10.1	11.5	11.5	11.5
(multiple of average earnings)	6.7	9.7	12.5	14.2	14.2	14.2
Net pension wealth	6.6	9.3	11.7	13.2	13.2	13.2
(multiple of average net earnings)	8.1	11.4	14.4	16.3	16.3	16.3

Turkey

An earnings-related public scheme with an income-tested safety net and a flat-rate supplementary pension.

Qualifying conditions

Recent entrants (from September 1999) can draw a pension from age 60 (men) or 58 (women) with 7 000 days of contributions. This is equivalent to around 28 years of contributions for continuous employment. An alternative eligibility condition is 25 years of insurance coverage with 4 500 days of contributions.

The means-tested pension is payable from age 65 only to those who are disabled or have no other social security rights.

Benefit calculation

Earnings-related

The pension under the new scheme is based on average lifetime earnings revalued in line with nominal GDP growth. The pension has a non-linear formula with years of coverage. The first 10 years earn a pension of 35% of pay, with 2% per year extra for the next 15 years and 1% per year thereafter.

There is a floor above which contributions are required. This had three different values during calendar 2002, varying between TRL 210 million at the beginning of the year and TRL 328 million at the end.

There is a ceiling to pensionable earnings; its value was TRL 1 050 million at the start of the year and TRL 1 638 million at the end of 2002.

The modelling uses the average of the variables above for the calendar year 2002.

Indexation of pensions in payment is to the consumer price index. Pensions are adjusted monthly.

Minimum

There is a minimum pension, which in 2002 varied between TRL 202 million and TRL 257 million.

Targeted

The means-tested pension is paid quarterly. For the first half of 2002 the pension was TRL 45 million per month, for the second, pension was TRL 49 million per month.

Pension modelling results: Turkey

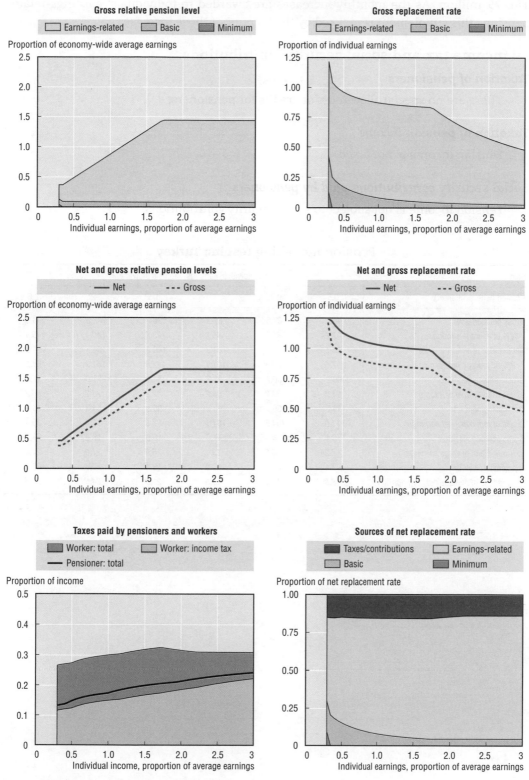

Source: OECD, based on information provided by the countries.

A monthly supplement is paid to all retirees. Its value started the year 2002 at TRL 75 million. As the monthly increases are awarded to individuals' earnings-related pensions this supplement is reduced by the amount of those increases.

Personal income tax and social security contributions

Taxation of pensioners

There are no special allowances or credits for pensioners.

Taxation of pension income

Pension income is not taxed.

Social security contributions paid by pensioners

Pension income is not subject to social security contributions.

Pension modelling results: Turkey

Men	Individual earnings, multiple of average					
Women (where different)	0.5	0.75	1	1.5	2	2.5
Gross pension level	48.1	67.6	87.2	126.2	143.8	143.8
(% of average earnings)	47.1	66.2	85.2	123.2	140.4	140.4
Net pension level	58.7	81.0	103.3	146.0	164.8	164.8
(% of average net earnings)	57.6	79.3	101.1	142.8	161.2	161.2
Gross replacement rate	96.2	90.2	87.2	84.1	71.9	57.5
(% of individual earnings)	94.2	88.2	85.2	82.2	70.2	56.2
Net replacement rate	113.2	106.7	103.3	99.9	84.3	66.8
(% of individual net earnings)	111.0	104.5	101.1	97.8	82.4	65.4
Gross pension wealth	6.1	8.5	11.0	15.9	18.2	18.2
(multiple of average earnings)	7.2	10.2	13.1	18.9	21.6	21.6
Net pension wealth	7.4	10.2	13.0	18.4	20.8	20.8
(multiple of average net earnings)	8.8	12.2	15.5	21.9	24.8	24.8

PENSIONS AT A GLANCE – ISBN 92-64-01871-9 – © OECD 2005

United Kingdom

Britain has a complex pension system, which mixes defined-benefit and defined-contribution formulae and public and private provision. The public scheme has two tiers (a flat-rate basic pension and an earnings-related additional pension), which are complemented by a large voluntary private pension sector. Most employee contributors "contract out" of the state second tier into private pensions of different sorts. A new income-related benefit (pension credit) has recently been introduced to target extra spending on the poorest pensioners.

Qualifying conditions

Pension age, currently 60 for women and 65 for men, will be equalised at 65 from 2010. The eligibility age for the minimum income guarantee/pension credit is 60, and will increase in line with the women's pension age. The new savings credit is only available from 65 for both men and women.

To qualify for the basic state pension, people need to pay social security contributions or have credits for around nine-tenths of their potential working lives (44 years). A proportionally reduced pension is available for people who do not meet the full condition, but only to a minimum of 25% (i.e., 11 years).

Benefit calculation

Basic

The full basic state pension for a single person was GBP 75.50 per week in 2002-03 (GBP 72.50 in 2001-02 giving an annual total for 2002 of GBP 3 896).

Earnings-related

The state second pension replaced the state earnings-related pension scheme (Serps) from 2002-03. This has a more redistributive schedule than its predecessor does. For earnings between the lower earnings limit (GBP 3 910 per year in 2002-03 and GBP 3 744 in 2001-02) and the first threshold (GBP 10 800, GBP 10 400), the replacement rate is 40% of the difference. This also applies to people covered by home responsibilities protection. This is equivalent to treating people earning below the first threshold as if they had earned at this level. Over the next range, the replacement rate is 10%, ending at GBP 24 650, GBP 23 710). Between this threshold and the ceiling, the replacement rate is 20%. The ceiling was GBP 30 505 in 2002-03 and GBP 29 900 in 2001-02.

The benefit value is calculated on average lifetime salary, with earlier years' pay uprated in line with average economy-wide earnings. The benefit is then price-indexed after retirement.

Pension modelling results: United Kingdom

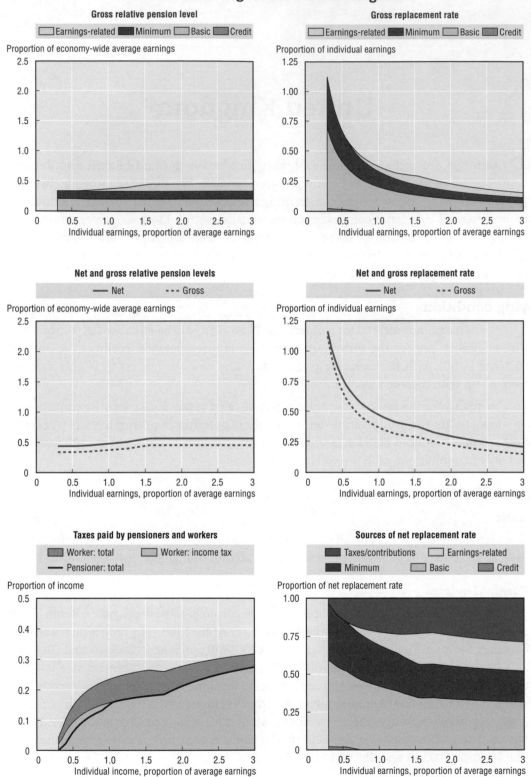

Source: OECD, based on information provided by the countries.

Contracting out

Some 55% of employees, however, are "contracted out" of the state second pension, into either an occupational plan (provided by an employer), a personal pension or a stakeholder plan (both provided by financial-services companies). Occupational schemes are mainly defined benefit, but there has been rapid growth since the mid-1980s in defined-contribution occupational plans, albeit from a very low base. The other plans are defined contribution.

Both employers and employees pay a lower rate of social security contributions when contracted out and the employee foregoes their state second pension entitlement. In return, defined-benefit schemes must meet minimum standards and defined-contribution plans must levy a minimum contribution.

The government sets the social security rebate, usually every five years, on the advice of the Government Actuary. The rebate is designed as fair compensation for the loss of state pension rights. As the Government Actuary's assumptions about investment returns and administrative costs are reasonable, the value of a contracted-out pension should be equivalent to the state benefit foregone. In a given year, around 45% of personal pension members contribute only the mandatory minimum to their plan.

Targeted

The minimum income guarantee (Mig) is, from 2003-04 onwards, converted into a "pension credit" which tops up low pensions. For consistency, the pension credit has been modelled using the 2002 calendar year parameters for the Mig. The target income level was GBP 98.15 per week for 2002-03 (GBP 92.15 for 2001-02) for a single person. The 2002 calendar year value for the Mig was GBP 5 041. There is no requirement to have paid social security contributions to receive Mig.

The pension credit also includes a new "savings credit" in addition to the "guarantee credit" that replaces the Mig. This is designed to reduce the effective withdrawal rate of benefits from 100% under the Mig to 40%. Individuals whose income (apart from the pension credit) is less than the target minimum income but more than a "starting point" receive a top up. The starting point is equal to the full value of the basic pension. The top up is 60% of income above the starting point. For people with incomes above the target minimum income, the benefit is reduced by 40% by the amount of the excess. The maximum credit for 2004-05 is therefore (GBP 105 – GBP 80) × 60% = GBP 15 per week.

Personal income tax and social security contributions

Taxation of pensioners

A single person under 65 had an income-tax allowance of GBP 4 615 per year in 2002-03, compared with GBP 6 100 for 65-74 year olds and GBP 6 370 for people 75 or over. Once a pensioner's total income exceeds GBP 17 900, the additional allowances are withdrawn at 50% of the excess, so that high-income pensioners have the same tax allowances as people of working age.

Taxation of pension income

No special reliefs are available for pension income.

Social security contributions paid by pensioners

Social security contributions are not levied on the income of those over state pension age.

Pension modelling results: United Kingdom

Men	Individual earnings, multiple of average					
Women (where different)	0.5	0.75	1	1.5	2	2.5
Gross pension level	33.7	34.8	37.1	43.9	45.1	45.1
(% of average earnings)						
Net pension level	43.6	44.9	47.6	55.1	56.3	56.3
(% of average net earnings)						
Gross replacement rate	67.4	46.4	37.1	29.3	22.5	18.0
(% of individual earnings)						
Net replacement rate	78.4	57.7	47.6	38.2	29.8	24.7
(% of individual net earnings)						
Gross pension wealth	5.0	5.2	5.5	6.6	6.7	6.7
(multiple of average earnings)	*5.8*	*6.0*	*6.4*	*7.5*	*7.7*	*7.7*
Net pension wealth	6.5	6.7	7.1	8.2	8.4	8.4
(multiple of average net earnings)	*7.5*	*7.7*	*8.2*	*9.4*	*9.6*	*9.6*

United States

The publicly provided pension benefit, known as social security, has a progressive benefit formula. There is also a means-tested top-up payment available for low-income pensioners.

Qualifying conditions

The current pension age (called normal retirement age, or NRA) is between 65 and 66, increasing to 67 in steps. Eligibility for retirement benefits depends on the number of years in which contributions are made with a minimum requirement of ten years' contributions. Early retirement is possible from 62 with reduced benefits.

Benefit calculation

Earnings-related

The benefit formula is progressive. The first USD 592 a month of relevant earnings attracts a 90% replacement rate. The band of earnings between USD 592 and USD 3 567 a month is replaced at 32%. These thresholds are 22 and 133% of average earnings, respectively. A replacement rate of 15% applies between the latter threshold and the earnings ceiling. A 50% dependants' addition is available to married couples where secondary earners have built up a smaller entitlement and for a qualifying dependent child.

Earlier years' earnings are revalued up to the year in which the recipient reaches age 60 in line with growth in economy-wide average earnings. There is no adjustment of all previous earnings between ages 60 and 62. Thereafter, previous earnings are adjusted in line with prices up to the age of 67. The benefit is based on the career average earnings for the 35 highest years of earnings (after revaluing) including years with zero earnings if needed to total 35 years. On the baseline assumptions for price and earnings growth this results in a benefit 14% lower than if all earnings were fully revalued in line with earnings.

The earnings ceiling for both contributions and benefits is USD 84 900 a year – 2½ times average earnings – uprated annually in line with growth in economy-wide earnings.

Pensions in payment are adjusted in line with prices.

Minimum

There is a minimum pension under social security. People earnings less than a special minimum primary insurance amount are given a minimum pension that depends on their lifetime total years of coverage, varying between USD 30 for 11 years' coverage and USD 626 for 30 years' coverage. The threshold for this minimum pension was USD 9 450 in 2002, or just under 30% of average earnings. (The threshold is defined formally as 15% of the "old law" contribution and benefit base.) The minimum pension does not affect the modelling results because the earnings range affected is below that presented.

Pension modelling results: United States

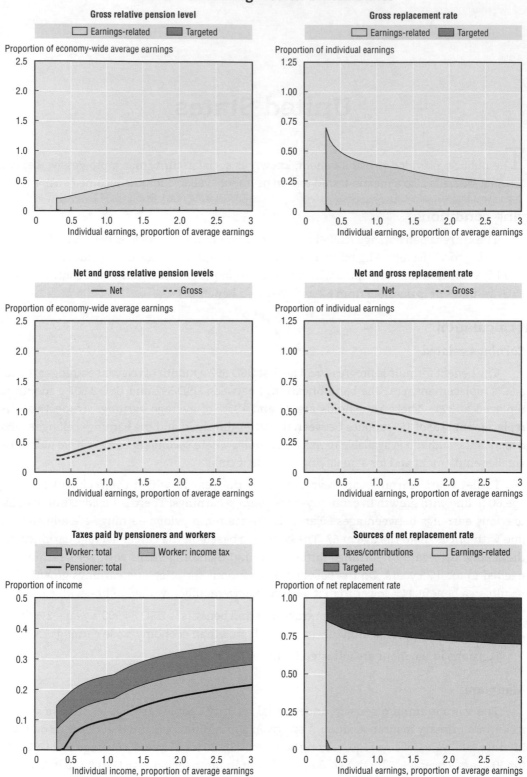

Source: OECD, based on information provided by the countries.

Targeted

The United States provide a means-tested benefit for the elderly, known as supplemental security income. Single people over the age of 65 can be eligible for up to USD 6 540 a year depending on assets and other income. The benefit rate for couples is USD 9 804 (50% higher than the rate for singles). These benefit rates are equivalent to around 20 and 29% of the national average wage, respectively. The benefit is indexed to prices.

The asset tests are strict: single people are limited to USD 2 000 worth of assets and couples to USD 3 000, excluding personal belongings, a home, a car, funeral insurance and life insurance (the last two up to USD 1 500 in value). There is a small (USD 20 a month) "disregard" in calculating the entitlement. The benefit is then withdrawn at a 100% rate against income above this level.

The analysis is complicated by the fact that states can supplement the federally determined minimum. While 12 states pay only the federal minimum, some 28 administer their own system and 12 offer supplements that are operated by the federal Social Security Administration. The average additional payment in these 12 states is 13% for single pensioners and 18% for couples. Note that the modelling does not include these additional payments.

Personal income tax and social security contributions

Taxation of pensioners

Older people are entitled to an additional standard deduction in the Federal income tax. For single people of working age, the deduction is USD 4 700 compared with USD 5 850 for the over 65s. A married couple in which both partners are over 65 is entitled to a deduction of USD 9 650, compared with a standard deduction of USD 7 850 for working-age couples. There is also a tax credit targeted on poorer pensioners and the disabled. The maximum credit is USD 1 125 for an individual (single head of household and widows and widowers), but this is withdrawn against income and is exhausted once total income exceeds USD 17 500 or non-taxable public pension benefits exceed USD 5 000.

Taxation of pension income

Up to one-half of social security (public-pension) benefits is taxable if income, including one half of the pension, exceeds USD 25 000. This proportion can increase to a maximum of 85% for higher-income pensioners if half of social security benefits plus other income exceeds USD 34 000.

Differences in personal-income-tax structures between states complicate analysis of the United States. For the main empirical results, we have followed the OECD standard methodology, which assumes that the example individual lives in Detroit, Michigan. The state income tax system for Michigan gives an extra tax-free allowance of USD 900 for people over age 65 (USD 1 800 for a married couple filing jointly). Public pensions are entirely exempt from the state income tax, as is the first USD 33 810 of income from a private pension. All income from pensions is exempt from the Detroit income tax. (Note that the chart for average effective tax rates does not show the negative figure for low-income workers' personal income tax due to the earned income credit although this is calculated and used in the modelling.)

Social security contributions paid by pensioners

No social security contributions are levied on pension income.

Pension modelling results: United States

Men	Individual earnings, multiple of average					
Women (where different)	0.5	0.75	1	1.5	2	2.5
Gross pension level	24.8	31.7	38.6	49.8	56.3	62.7
(% of average earnings)						
Net pension level	32.7	41.9	51.0	63.0	69.8	77.1
(% of average net earnings)						
Gross replacement rate	49.6	42.3	38.6	33.2	28.1	25.1
(% of individual earnings)						
Net replacement rate	61.4	54.6	51.0	44.9	39.0	35.5
(% of individual net earnings)						
Gross pension wealth	3.5	4.5	5.5	7.1	8.0	8.9
(multiple of average earnings)	*4.1*	*5.3*	*6.4*	*8.3*	*9.3*	*10.4*
Net pension wealth	4.7	6.0	7.3	9.0	9.9	11.0
(multiple of average net earnings)	*5.4*	*6.9*	*8.5*	*10.5*	*11.6*	*12.8*

ISBN 92-64-01871-9
Pensions at a Glance
Public Policies across OECD Countries
© OECD 2005

VOLUNTARY, OCCUPATIONAL PENSIONS

Occupational pension schemes, voluntarily provided by employers, are common in many OECD countries. This section shows detailed results on the value of these pension entitlements for four countries: Canada, Denmark, the United Kingdom and the United States. These four countries were chosen for three reasons. First, coverage of occupational pensions is broad: around one third of employees in Canada, a little under half in the United Kingdom and the United States and around 80% in Denmark.[1] Secondly, occupational pensions play an important role in providing retirement incomes. Thirdly, data are available on the rules and parameters of different employers' plans for these countries.[2, 3]

The analysis of the four countries that follows is presented in the same format as the country studies that discuss mandatory pension systems. These provide detailed descriptions of the rules and parameters chosen for the representative pension plan and the justification for that choice. The table below offers a cross-country summary of these provisions for the three countries where defined-benefit pension systems have been modelled. In Denmark, occupational pensions are of the defined-contribution type.

It is also important to note that defined-benefit occupational plans often have more generous rules for age of retirement than do national programmes. For comparison with other countries and with the results of mandatory pensions only, it is again assumed that people retire at the normal pension age of the public scheme. In practice, earlier retirement will result in lower benefits because of the smaller number of years over which pension accrues.

Parameters and rules for defined-benefit occupational pensions

	Canada	United Kingdom	United States
Earnings measure	Final salary (70%)	Final salary (95%)	Final salary (55%)
Vesting	5 years' service	2 years' service	5 years' service
Pension age	65	65	65 (47%)
Accrual rate	2% a year (70%)	1.25% a year (65%)	1.5% a year
Integration method	1.3% accrual up to public ceiling	–	–
Pre-retirement preservation	None	Price inflation	None
Post-retirement benefit adjustment	Half price inflation	Price inflation	None

Notes

1. See OECD (2001), Table 6.2 and Johnson (1998), Table 3.3.

2. The data for Canada come from OECD (1995). For the United Kingdom, data are drawn principally from the National Association of Pension Funds annual survey. The Government Actuary's survey is published with a huge delay, with 1995 data only available in 2001. Disney and Whitehouse (1994, 1996) provide simulations of pension entitlements for a range of different scheme rules and parameters. Data for the United States come mainly from Mitchell and Dykes (2000), which is based on a survey of schemes by the Department of Labor; see also Department of Labor (1999).

3. In other countries with broad coverage of occupational pensions – such as Germany, Japan and Switzerland – there have been no surveys of employer pension plans. It is impossible, therefore, to model with any degree of certainty the rules of a "typical" scheme.

Canada

Over 40% of the Canadian workforce are members of occupational pension schemes, known as retirement pension plans. Around 45% of this total are members of public sector schemes. This gives a coverage rate in the private sector of around 30% compared with nearly 100% coverage among public-sector employees.

There was a shift to defined-contribution schemes in the 1980s and 1990s in the private sector, but these plans still account for just 13% of total members (including hybrid plans with defined-benefit and defined-contribution elements). Over 60% of members are in final-salary defined-benefit schemes, with 10% in schemes with an average-salary formula and 20% in plans that provide a flat benefit for each year of membership. Most schemes cover the entire workforce, but 20% of members are in schemes reserved solely for members of trades unions.

Most occupational schemes – covering 90% of members – are compulsory for people eligible to join. Typically, eligibility is determined by years of service (to a legal maximum of two years). Vesting rules vary by province, but are generally two years of membership or five years' service. Some also depend on age. Pensions can be transferred to another occupational scheme or a personal plan when a worker changes jobs, or "preserved" in the old occupational scheme until an employee reaches pension age.

Pension age is generally 65, but a significant minority of public-sector members can claim their pension at 60. The accrual rate in public sector schemes is nearly always 2% of earnings for each year of service. The earnings formula is usually based on the best five years. In the private sector, 2% is also the most common accrual rate, accounting for nearly half of members. But almost a third have accrual rates between 1½ and 2% and another 10% between 1 and 1½% per year of service. There has been a shift towards the norm of 2% accrual, partly because this is the maximum allowed by income-tax regulations.

Most schemes are integrated with the public earnings-related scheme, giving a lower accrual rate (usually 1.3 to 1.5%) on the slice of earnings up to the ceiling for the second-tier pension. Lump-sum benefits are not permitted.

In 1989, post-retirement indexation was automatic for 70% of members of public-sector schemes, but only for 7.5% in the private sector. However, only 28% of public sector members were guaranteed full inflation uprating. Most large schemes, however, provided for *ad hoc* increases that compensate for about half of inflation.

Pension modelling results with voluntary schemes: Canada

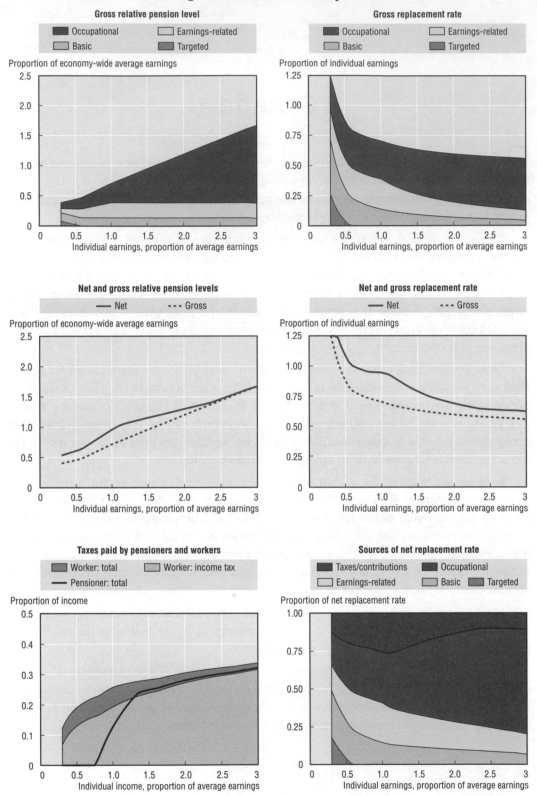

Source: OECD, based on information provided by the countries.

Pension modelling results: Canada, with voluntary occupational plans

Men	Individual earnings, multiple of average					
Women (where different)	0.5	0.75	1	1.5	2	2.5
Gross pension level	44.1	56.1	70.3	94.6	118.9	143.2
(% of average earnings)						
Net pension level	59.4	75.5	94.6	114.4	129.0	145.6
(% of average net earnings)						
Gross replacement rate	88.2	74.8	70.3	63.1	59.4	57.3
(% of individual earnings)						
Net replacement rate	108.9	96.4	94.6	78.8	68.8	63.7
(% of individual net earnings)						
Gross pension wealth	6.5	8.2	10.2	13.5	16.8	20.1
(multiple of average earnings)	*7.5*	*9.5*	*11.8*	*15.6*	*19.4*	*23.2*
Net pension wealth	8.7	11.0	13.7	16.3	18.2	20.4
(multiple of average net earnings)	*10.1*	*12.7*	*15.9*	*18.9*	*21.1*	*23.6*

Denmark

Defined-contribution schemes are agreed between the social partners. Coverage is almost universal. Contributions to these schemes are typically between 9% and 17% of earnings. Benefits are usually withdrawn as an annuity, although some schemes allow for lump-sum payments. Annuity calculations are based on an assumed interest rate, which is 1.5% for recent contributions and schemes (although was previously 4.5%). However, the schemes operate on a "with-profit" or "participating" basis. This means that pension increases depend on the investment performance of the fund and the mortality experience of its beneficiaries. Since 2000, all negotiated schemes must use unisex life tables for calculating pension values.

The modelling assumes the lowest contribution rate of 9% and calculates a price indexed annuity based on a real discount rate of 1.5%.

Pension modelling results: Denmark, with voluntary occupational plans

Men	Individual earnings, multiple of average					
Women (where different)	0.5	0.75	1	1.5	2	2.5
Gross pension level	56.7	63.7	70.8	84.8	102.2	122.4
(% of average earnings)						
Net pension level	68.5	75.5	82.4	96.1	109.9	124.2
(% of average net earnings)						
Gross replacement rate	113.3	85.0	70.8	56.6	51.1	48.9
(% of individual earnings)						
Net replacement rate	125.0	96.9	82.4	72.5	66.6	62.8
(% of individual net earnings)						
Gross pension wealth	9.3	10.2	11.2	13.1	15.6	18.6
(multiple of average earnings)	*10.4*	*11.3*	*12.3*	*14.2*	*16.1*	*19.1*
Net pension wealth	11.2	12.1	13.0	14.9	16.8	18.9
(multiple of average net earnings)	*12.6*	*13.5*	*14.4*	*16.2*	*18.0*	*20.1*

Pension modelling results with voluntary schemes: Denmark

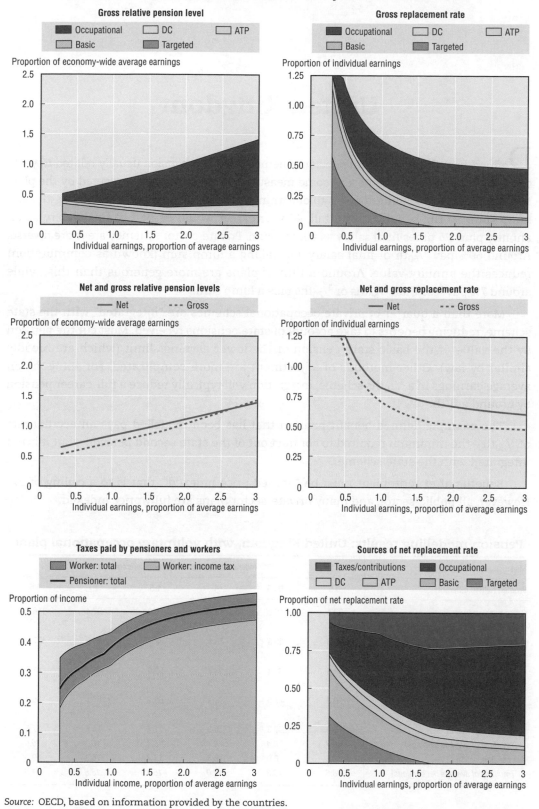

Source: OECD, based on information provided by the countries.

United Kingdom

$\mathbf{D}$efined-benefit occupational pension schemes provide a pension usually related to years of membership of the scheme and some measure of final salary when covered by the plan. Most public-sector schemes pay $^1/_{80}$th of earnings per year of membership, plus $^3/_{80}$ths as a lump sum. So the benefit after a full, 40-year career would be half of final salary as an annuity plus 1½ times final salary as a lump sum. Private-sector schemes are more diverse. Around 60% pay $^1/_{60}$th of final salary. But taking a lump sum (known as commutation) reduces the annuity value. Around a fifth of plans are more generous than this, while around 7% pay less than $^1/_{60}$ths or $^1/_{80}$ths plus a lump sum.

More than a quarter of private occupational schemes are "integrated" with the state scheme, reducing benefits to take account of state pensions received. Most cut the pension by the value of the basic state pension or the lower earnings limit (which are broadly similar by law). Other methods of adjustment are more complicated. For someone on average earnings in a $^1/_{60}$ths scheme, integration will typically reduce a full-career pension by around a fifth.

The example defined-benefit pension that has been modelled pays an accrual rate of $^1/_{80}$th – the minimum required to contract out of the state second pension – but it is not integrated with the state scheme.

Benefits after retirement must be "limited price indexed", that is to a ceiling of 5%. However, all public-sector, and many private-sector plans are fully price indexed.

Pension modelling results: United Kingdom, with voluntary occupational plans

Men	Individual earnings, multiple of average					
Women (where different)	0.5	0.75	1	1.5	2	2.5
Gross pension level	39.4	49.1	58.7	78.0	97.4	116.7
(% of average earnings)						
Net pension level	50.3	60.3	70.1	89.8	108.5	127.0
(% of average net earnings)						
Gross replacement rate	78.8	65.4	58.7	52.0	48.7	46.7
(% of individual earnings)						
Net replacement rate	90.3	77.5	70.1	62.2	57.5	55.7
(% of individual net earnings)						
Gross pension wealth	5.9	7.3	8.8	11.7	14.6	17.5
(multiple of average earnings)	6.7	8.4	10.1	13.4	16.7	20.0
Net pension wealth	7.5	9.0	10.5	13.4	16.2	19.0
(multiple of average net earnings)	8.6	10.3	12.0	15.4	18.6	21.8

Pension modelling results with voluntary schemes: United Kingdom

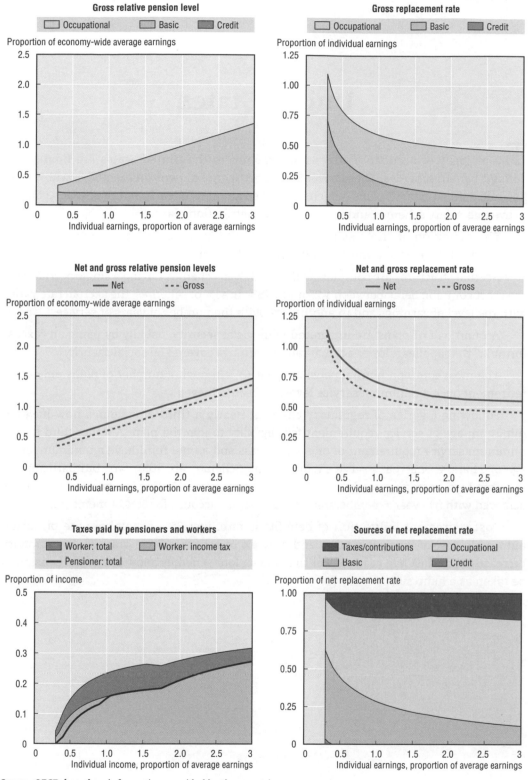

Gross relative pension level

☐ Occupational   ☐ Basic   ■ Credit

Proportion of economy-wide average earnings

Individual earnings, proportion of average earnings

Gross replacement rate

☐ Occupational   ☐ Basic   ■ Credit

Proportion of individual earnings

Individual earnings, proportion of average earnings

Net and gross relative pension levels

—— Net   --- Gross

Proportion of economy-wide average earnings

Individual earnings, proportion of average earnings

Net and gross replacement rate

—— Net   --- Gross

Proportion of individual earnings

Individual earnings, proportion of average earnings

Taxes paid by pensioners and workers

■ Worker: total   ☐ Worker: income tax
—— Pensioner: total

Proportion of income

Individual income, proportion of average earnings

Sources of net replacement rate

■ Taxes/contributions   ☐ Occupational
☐ Basic   ■ Credit

Proportion of net replacement rate

Individual earnings, proportion of average earnings

Source: OECD, based on information provided by the countries.

United States

The majority of occupational pension schemes in the United States are final-salary defined-benefit schemes. These cover 56% of occupational pension members, with 23% in flat-rate defined-benefit plans (which pay a fixed amount for each month of coverage), 11% in average-salary schemes and 6% in defined-contribution plans.

The definition of "final salary" varies, but the most common formula is the best consecutive five years' earnings, accounting for 65% of members.

Accrual structures are complex, with only 37% in schemes having a single accrual rate, the most common being between 1.25 and 1.75%. In 41% of schemes, the accrual rate varies with the level of earnings and in another 8%, with the number of years of service.

Around half of plans are integrated with social security, usually by using an "excess formula" that applies a lower accrual rate to earnings covered by social security.

The most common normal pension age is 65, although a number of plans only allow retirement once a minimum service level has been achieved.

Following a series of regulatory changes, nearly a third of schemes now have no minimum age or service requirement for eligibility to join the plan. Another third have a minimum service requirement of one year or less and a final third have a minimum entry age of 21 and a one-year's-service requirement. Schemes are voluntary, but participation rates are high, averaging nearly 80% of full-time employees. Vesting is now most commonly achieved with five year's membership: these schemes account for 85% of members.

Post-retirement indexation of benefits is rare: just 3% of members are promised automatic cost-of-living increases and only 4% of schemes have granted discretionary increases in the last five years. Fewer than one in four schemes allow any of the pension to be taken as a lump sum.

Pension modelling results with voluntary schemes: United States

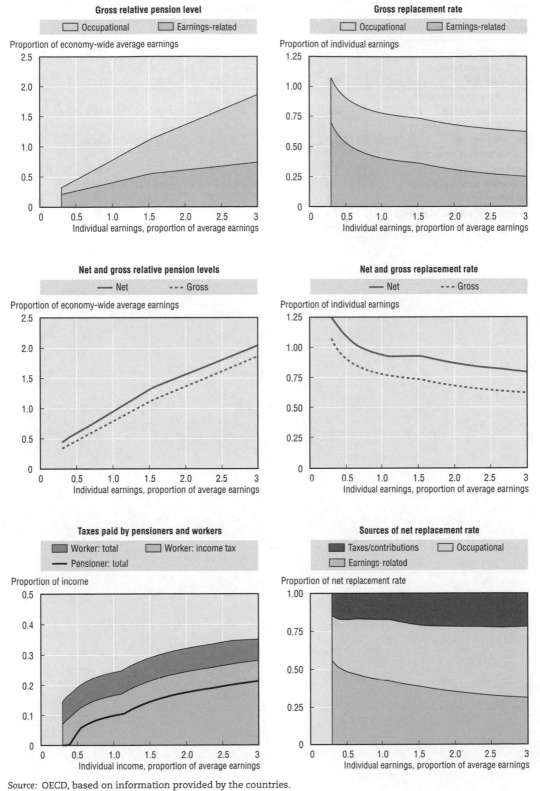

Gross relative pension level

☐ Occupational   ▨ Earnings-related

Proportion of economy-wide average earnings

Gross replacement rate

☐ Occupational   ▨ Earnings-related

Proportion of individual earnings

Net and gross relative pension levels

—— Net   - - - Gross

Proportion of economy-wide average earnings

Net and gross replacement rate

—— Net   - - - Gross

Proportion of individual earnings

Taxes paid by pensioners and workers

▨ Worker: total   ☐ Worker: income tax
—— Pensioner: total

Proportion of income

Individual income, proportion of average earnings

Sources of net replacement rate

▨ Taxes/contributions   ☐ Occupational
▧ Earnings-related

Proportion of net replacement rate

Individual earnings, proportion of average earnings

Source: OECD, based on information provided by the countries.

Pension modelling results: United States, with voluntary occupational plans

Men	Individual earnings, multiple of average					
Women (where different)	0.5	0.75	1	1.5	2	2.5
Gross pension level	43.4	59.7	75.9	105.8	130.9	156.0
(% of average earnings)						
Net pension level	56.3	73.7	91.9	125.4	151.0	175.2
(% of average net earnings)						
Gross replacement rate	86.9	79.6	75.9	70.5	65.5	62.4
(% of individual earnings)						
Net replacement rate	105.7	96.1	91.9	89.3	84.2	80.6
(% of individual net earnings)						
Gross pension wealth	5.7	7.7	9.8	13.5	16.6	19.7
(multiple of average earnings)	*6.6*	*8.9*	*11.3*	*15.6*	*19.1*	*22.6*
Net pension wealth	7.4	9.5	11.9	16.0	19.1	22.1
(multiple of average net earnings)	*8.5*	*11.0*	*13.7*	*18.5*	*22.1*	*25.4*